"This is one of the best dating books I've ever read. *The Automatic 2nd Date gives you the tools to explore what you really need out of a relationship and shows you how to unlock your special sparkle within. Had I known these skills at a younger age, I would have been married ten years earlier."*

—Lynn Rosenthal, TV producer, recovered date-a-holic

"*Pull up a chair and lean in. You are about to discover the secret truths of dating successfully and finding the real you along the way. This book could change everything for you."*

—Tammy Trent, recording artist, author, speaker

"*Do you want the honest truth on making a positive first impression? Sensible, practical, and intuitive, this is the perfect handbook for success for building healthy and meaningful dating relationships."*

—Karol Ladd, bestselling author of *The Power of a Positive Woman*

"*Automatic 2nd hit! Victorya hooked me on the first page! I especially love the recap points and journaling at the end of each chapter. Great job, Victorya! No wonder you're married to such an amazing man!"*

—Karen Covell, author, TV producer,
founding director of Hollywood Prayer Network
www.Hollywoodprayernetwork.org

"*If you want the self-esteem, self-confidence, and courage to attract and keep the man that you and your mother always wanted for you, this is the book for you. With her magical communication style, Victorya shows you how to become the person you've really been all along."*

—Pamela J. Bolen, licensed professional counselor

"*Every single woman and every mother of a single daughter must read* The Automatic 2nd Date! *It's brimming with great advice from a dating expert, for yourself or to pass on to someone you love."*

—Susan Wales, author of *A Match Made in Heaven I & II*

everything to
say and do
on the 1st date
to guarantee . . .

the *2automatic*
nd date

VICTORYA MICHAELS
ROGERS

HOWARD BOOKS
A DIVISION OF SIMON & SCHUSTER
New York   London   Toronto   Sydney

Our purpose at Howard Books is to:
- *Increase faith* in the hearts of growing Christians
- *Inspire holiness* in the lives of believers
- *Instill hope* in the hearts of struggling people everywhere

Because He's coming again!

Howard Books, a division of Simon & Schuster, Inc.
1230 Avenue of the Americas, New York, NY 10020
HOWARD www.howardpublishing.com
BOOKS

The Automatic 2nd Date © 2007 by Victorya Michaels Rogers

First Howard trade paperback edition October 2007

HOWARD and colophon are registered trademarks of Simon & Schuster, Inc.

For information regarding special discounts for bulk purchases, please contact Simon & Schuster Special Sales at 1-800-456-6798 or business@simonandschuster.com.

Edited by Philis Boultinghouse
Cover design by Terry Dugan Designs
Interior design by Davina Mock-Maniscalco
Author photo by Steve Riley Pictures
Cover image by Alamy/Tetra Images

Manufactured in the United States of America

10 9 8 7 6 5 4 3 2 1

Library of Congress Cataloging-in-Publication Data

Rogers, Victorya Michaels.
      The automatic 2nd date : everything to say and do on the 1st date to guarantee . . . / Victorya Michaels Rogers.
      p. cm.
      Summary: "Step-by-step advice on how to behave before, during, and after a date in order to compel the man you want to call back"—Provided by publisher.
      1. Dating (Social customs) 2. Man-woman relationships.
   I. Title. II. Title: Automatic second date.
      HQ801.R6335 2007
      646.7′7082—dc22   2007016056

ISBN 13: 978-1-4165-4382-4
ISBN 10:   1-4165-4382-1

I dedicate this book to every one of you single gals who has ever been disappointed in your dating life— be it trying to find the next first date or bewildered as to why you didn't get the second.
Things are about to change!

Contents

Acknowledgments ix

Introduction xi

1. The Magnetic Woman:
   The Art of First Impressions 1

2. The Eye of the Beholder:
   Presenting Your Best Outer Self 32

3. Your Male GPS: *How and Where to Meet Men* 59

4. A Little Help from My Friends:
   Welcome to the World of Blind Dates and Setups 89

5. Clueless No More: *Tips for That First Conversation* 111

6. On Your Mark, Get Set . . . :
   Getting Ready for That First Date 127

7. You Had Me at Hello:
   Conversation Tips for the First Date 149

8. Let the Sparks Fly!: *How to Connect on Date One* 172

9. To Kiss or Not to Kiss: *How to Say Goodnight* 190

10. After the First Date, Just Breathe: *Playing It Cool*   211

Epilogue:
After the Second Date: Keep Him Pursuing You   229

Addendum: *Discovering Who You Are:*
Finding Your True Worth   233

Notes   247

Acknowledgments

This book would never have been written without the prayers and support of my amazing family and friends. Here's to my most cherished cheerleaders!

To my husband, Will, thanks for giving me that ever-important second date, for allowing me to share my dating past with the world, and for continuing to be the man of my dreams.

To my kids, Matthew and Katie, thanks for tolerating Mommy keeping her laptop attached to her seemingly at every waking moment.

To my mom, Sandra Sterud, and my sister, Teri Rippeon, thanks for consistent daily phone calls and for helping me re-live so many of those, hmm, shall I say, memorable first dates.

To my mother-in-law, Pat Rogers, this has been a painful year for you and yet you were there to love my babies, read my pages, and clean my house in the midst of it all. Thank you.

To Kelly Free, Amy Wahman, Lori Beeman, and Karen Covell, thanks for continuing to be there for me—you kept me going each time I called to whine about once again facing a blank page with a blank stare.

To Philis Boultinghouse, thanks for choosing to edit this one for me. I so appreciate your believing in me and pushing me onward during both the writing and editing phase of this book. It has been a challenging time in both our lives, to say the least, and what a blessing to walk with you through it.

To Melissa Teutsch for being a great publicist and friend. It was great to travel and work with you on *Finding a Man Worth Keeping,* and I'm already enjoying working with you again on *The Automatic 2nd Date.* (Hey, isn't motherhood the absolute best!)

To John and Chrys Howard, Denny Boultinghouse, and the entire Howard Books family, thanks for believing in me and my vision.

Last, but not least, thanks to my Lord and Savior Jesus Christ. I am in awe of the undeserved and amazing life You've given me. What a privilege to be allowed to use my past, pain, and life lessons to improve the lives of others—it has brought value to each tear I've ever shed.

Introduction

What is the mystery about getting men to call back? You go out, seem to have a great time, he says he'll call you, and then nothing, zippo, silence. He's gone. What is wrong with this picture? Why does dating have to be so hard? Isn't there such a thing as falling in like? And is falling in love an impossible dream? Are all men lying jerks? Worse yet, yikes, could it be that you are scaring all the guys away without even knowing it?

If you have felt that "Losers" with a capital *L* are lurking everywhere, even in church, so much so that you actually catch yourself telling folks, "All men are jerks," or "There's just no one out there for me," then I'm about to make your day. There are great guys out there who can and will ask you out for a second date! Not only will I teach you how to cause men to want to ask you out, I'm going to teach you how to transform yourself into an intriguing, fun, magnetic woman who actually enjoys the entire dating process!

Why must you learn what I'm about to teach you? Because the harsh reality is that if you can't get a man to call you back for a second date, you will not be shopping for solitaire rings anytime soon! *The Automatic 2nd Date* opens your life up to new realities by revealing proven, hands-on, step-by-step instructions on how to behave before, during, and after a first date in order to compel your man to call you for that ever-important second date. Yes, I am about to teach you the skills needed to dramatically improve your appeal and popularity with the opposite sex, all while keeping your dignity and self-respect intact! Honest.

I've written *The Automatic 2nd Date* for every woman who has ever lain in bed wondering why "he" didn't call back. You may be a teenager or college student. You may be from Generation X or the baby-boomer generation. You could be brand-new to dating or a battle-worn veteran at a loss as to why you're getting less than favorable results. Perhaps you are unexpectedly single again following a divorce or the death of a spouse, and you find yourself back in a game from which you were long removed. Do you feel you don't have a clue where to start? If any of these scenarios describes you, read on. You've picked up the right book.

The Science of Dating

During my single years, I spent a decade as a Hollywood agent. During this time, I was pursued by a rock star, a movie star, a gospel singer, a navy pilot, a doctor, a salesman, an accountant, a fireman, a police officer, a preacher, and an athlete before I finally caught my Mr. Wonderful. In fact, during one eighteen-month period, I went out with more than one hundred blind dates and setups—98 percent asking me for a second date, *and* I didn't go Dutch treat on any of these dates. I had dating down to a science. I'm writing this book to teach that science to you. Follow my advice, and you will save yourself not only time and frustration, but hopefully you'll miss out on a lot of needless heartache from miscommunication.

I didn't happen upon these secrets easily or through some epiphany or nighttime vision. It took years of heartache, prayer, research, rejection, and practice, practice, practice. You see, I had a slow start in the dating world. Throughout high school and college, I was clueless about dating. I was the cute guys' buddy, not the girl they asked out on Friday night.

Not only were dates few and far between, but when I *did* get asked out, second dates were far from guaranteed. I was nervous, clumsy, and tongue-tied. All too often I spent weekend nights as a dateless dreamer. Does this sound familiar?

Over and over I begged God for answers. What was I doing wrong? "Hey, I'm a nice person. I'm not *that* ugly. Why doesn't anyone want me?"

After getting my bachelor's degree in broadcast journalism with a minor in speech communication, opportunities came my way to work my way up the ladder of success in Hollywood. By twenty-three, I was promoted to talent agent in the movie and television business, representing writers, producers, directors, actors, and technical crews.

While I thoroughly enjoyed meeting gorgeous celebrities like Brad Pitt, Jon Bon Jovi, and Kevin Costner (I mean, who wouldn't?), it occurred to me that it was models and glamorous actresses I ought to be observing for lessons in romance. I studied the way they walked, talked, and dressed. I paid attention to their body language and eye movements when they were around desirable men. I was on a mission to become a bachelor magnet, just like these ladies. I mean, these women effortlessly drew men to themselves merely by walking into the room and glancing a man's way. I wanted to do that.

I had embarked on a serious journey. I began reading every dating and relating book I could get my hands on, and I attended all kinds of relationship seminars by experts both in and out of the church. I put the good advice into practice and discarded the ridiculous or demoralizing stuff. The absurd advice seemed easy for me to identify, as I was blessed with parents who instilled in me strong Christian values that ran all the way to the core of my being.

I listened, I observed, and then I put into practice what I gleaned from the many influences in my daily life. I was learning from fashion models, glamorous actresses, bestselling authors, relationship experts, and a handful of wise pastors. It paid off. Surviving embarrassing moments, immature expectations, and plenty of mistakes, I grabbed enough success to keep me in the game. I began to learn everything a girl needs to do or say on a first date to get an automatic second date (while still respecting herself in the morning).

When I mastered the first date, second dates became automatic. I would end an evening with a new man and just know that I'd hear back within three days with a request for another date.

I had mastered the skills of authentic one-on-one communication with someone new—skills, by the way, that also work outside the romance arena, including business, social, and any interpersonal relationship with both male and female. Not only did my business life soar from these new social skills, but my platonic friendships improved as well. I had learned to pay attention to others rather than merely focusing on myself!

By my late twenties, when I found myself still without a husband, I decided to expand my playing field and asked most anyone around me to actively get involved in my love life by making introductions and setting me up on blind dates. During the eighteen months that followed, someone, somewhere would set me up with a new man more than one hundred times, and the first-date skills I had developed from all my research continued to prove their merit. That was the time period when 98 percent of my first dates asked me out for a second.

Just a Game?

Was game playing involved in getting nearly one hundred guys to call me for a second date? That's a matter of interpretation. Some may have called it game playing, but it was never a frivolous game. It was serious sport and smart sense! Let me clarify which definition of "game" we are talking about.

Webster defines "game" several ways. I am *not* referring to the kind of game that is an "activity engaged in for diversion or amusement." Rather, I'm referring to "a procedure or strategy for gaining an end; a tactic." [1]

Business is a game; personal relationships are a game. Even *life* is a game. The game we're striving to win is love. If you're going to enter the game, do it to win. Otherwise, why bother? One of the most inspired writers of all time put it this way: "You've all been to the stadium and seen the athletes race. Everyone runs; one wins. Run to win. All good athletes train hard" (St. Paul). [2]

Winning takes perseverance, passion, and persistence; but you can master all three strategies because somewhere inside you know you're worth it! *The Automatic 2nd Date* will help you train for your race to the finish line of an invigorating dating life.

Develop the relational skills that I'll teach you in the pages ahead, and you will improve in all areas of your interpersonal life! So yes, just like sports, business, and war, love is a game. But unlike many games, the game of love is infinitely worthwhile.

There's a saying I used often during my dating years: "Like tennis, I just can't get into a game where love means nothing."

And I tell you, love *means* something. It means everything. So take it seriously, even on a first date.

Step by Step

Find a cozy seat, and let's dig in as you learn everything to do and say on a first date to get that second. In chapter 1, we master the art of first impressions as we become magnetic. To get that date, he has to notice you. You are about to transform yourself into a magnet for the opposite sex from the moment you cross his path.

We continue this mission in chapter 2 as you become the beholder of your own beauty. You'll discover your beauty, minimize your flaws, and get ready to present your best self to the world of available men.

Chapter 3 is where the action begins when we turn on our Male GPS and go where the men are. You'll expand your horizons, find out what you like and don't like, and enjoy your vast new "meet" market. We continue exploring that meet market in chapter 4 by enlisting a little help from your friends. The quickest way to increase your access to quality men is to ask your friends to make the introductions. Welcome to the world of blind dates and setups. Dating will never be the same.

By chapter 5, it's time to cover the first phone call or in-person chitchat to compel your man to actually ask you out on that date. You will learn how to sail through that conversation with ease and charm. Plus you'll learn how to relay the unspoken message that you're popular, hard to get, and must be booked early if he wants you. By the chapter's end, you'll no longer be clueless about the ins and outs of those nerve-wracking moments.

Chapter 6 put us at the starting line of our race to the automatic second date. On your mark, get set, let's dive into the details of your first date, including dress code, Plan B, and running into friends.

Chapter 7 will be your best friend because I'll teach you how to grab him at hello. Covered here is everything you need to say or ask during your date, including one hundred questions you can ask your man.

In chapter 8, we learn how to get the sparks flying, as you connect with your man. You'll learn how to instantly put him at ease and convince him you are the right gal for him. On top of teaching the art of flattery and laughter, you'll learn a little-known yet powerful skill that subconsciously draws your man to you.

Chapter 9 cuts to the chase—to kiss or not to kiss. Not only do we cover your first good-bye in detail, we also answer the question everyone wants to know: how far can you go on a first date to get him to call you back, while still respecting yourself in the morning?

Finally, we get to life after the first date in chapter 10, including what you do while you're waiting to hear from your man.

At the end of each chapter, you'll find two special features:

1. An Automatic Recap—this highlights the main points from the chapter so you can review them quickly whenever you need to refresh your memory or give yourself a boost of motivation.

2. Automatic Journaling prompts—here you'll find several suggestions to encourage you to "untangle" your thoughts by allowing them to flow through a pen and onto a piece of paper. Thinking things through enough to write them down can help you actually make a plan and then act on that plan. Throughout the book, you'll also find miscellaneous suggestions for journaling, besides what's at the end of the chapter; so keep that journal and pen handy and ready to help you think and plan and *dream*.

Warning, Warning, Warning!

I must warn you, these secrets work on both good boys *and* bad boys, so you need to pay attention to all you learn about your date so you can figure out which category he falls into. Just as there are great guys out there whom you have not yet met, there are bad guys too—losers, controllers, love-'em-and-leave-'em heartbreakers, actors, moochers, users, and abusers. These secrets work on them as well, so learn to discern so you can weed them out by the end of the first date.

Pay special attention to your date's words and body language when you're together! Believe me, I'm confident Kevin Federline was quite open about his life goals and values early on in his relationship with Britney Spears, yet the young Spears let her attraction to his confidence and outward appearance blind her to obvious warning signs of a less than loyal and nurturing mate. Bad boys may be fun for excitement and notches in your lipstick case, but they leave you feeling empty and unfulfilled. So pay attention and proceed with caution. Know what you want before the date; and if your date falls under the bad-boy category, it's up to you to have the brains to say no for the second date when your head is still in more control than your heart.

So pull out your highlighter, and get ready to step out with the new you! You are beginning a covert race of chasing your man until he catches you! Whether you're ready for marriage or merely ready to enjoy a more active dating life, fasten your seatbelt and get ready for the ride of your life! If you master these skills, your man may never know you saw him first. At the very least, you will see your repeat-date ratio skyrocket. Enjoy the ride and keep your eyes open.

The Magnetic Woman

The Art of First Impressions

It has been reflected in countless variations throughout the history of the TV sitcom. You've seen it in *The Flying Nun* with Sally Field, *That Girl* with Marlo Thomas, *Sex and the City* with Sarah Jessica Parker, even *Friends* with Jennifer Aniston, Courteney Cox, and Lisa Kudrow.

You know what I'm talking about—some girl or girls are fumbling and frolicking through sprinklers or parks or big cities, effortlessly ready to take on the world. These gals are full of charisma, clumsiness, charm, and a confidence that exudes from their skinny pores as they skip, splash, twirl, and laugh. They are having fun, they are infectious, and men are falling in love with them.

Come on now, give me a break. I mean, let's be honest. Doesn't all their charming adorableness just make you want to gag?

Maybe, perhaps, just a little? If you've just nodded your head, then, girlfriend, you have come to the right place. Because even though watching them may churn our stomachs, deep down we all feel a twinge of jealously at their ability to effortlessly and completely attract men.

Well, I'm here to tell you that you have the same magnetic personality of these perky TV characters somewhere inside you, and I'm going to show you how to find it. You *have* to find it, or all the secrets I'm about to share about gaining that automatic second date will be wasted. You see, if you can't attract a *first* date, there won't be any second dates, forget about automatic. So with this book in hand, collapse into your most comfortable chair, snuggle up with a cozy blanket, and allow me to help you discover your own authentic, personal magnetism.

You've Got It in You

You are about to learn how to compel any man to walk right on over and ask you out. Sound impossible? Not when you've mastered the art of first impressions and tapped in to your magnetic self.

mag·net·ic
Possessing an extraordinary power or ability to attract
<a *magnetic* personality>[1]

Hey, I used to be that insecure, dateless girl. If *I* was able to push through my fear, learn to laugh at all my clumsiness, and emerge as a magnetic woman, then so can you!

The Impact of First Impressions

Becoming magnetic definitely includes etching that indelible mark on another's mind when you first come into his presence. Those ever-important first impressions are made within seconds. Experts differ on the exact percentage of how much of that first impression is your body language, how much is your appearance, and how much is your audible communication. But what they do agree on is that it's more about your body language and appearance than your actual words.

Cutting to the chase, people size you up the minute they see you, making a lasting assessment of your worth long before you even open your mouth. This assessment is based on your body language (stance, posture, expressions, and gestures) plus your appearance (hairstyle, clothing, physique, and perceived beauty). All these elements make up your overall nonverbal presentation. The assessments made in those first few seconds are rarely accurate, but they are believed to be true unless or until they are proven otherwise.

How's that for unfair pressure? It's not that this is news to you, right? But hold on a minute—just because you haven't graced the cover of a magazine doesn't mean you can't make memorable first impressions. No way, José. Inside of you right now is everything you need to transform your first impressions into magnetically positive memories.

Begin with *Your* Impression of You

Change the way you see yourself, and you'll change the way others see you. Your perception of *you* affects every part of your outward presentation, from the vibe you put out to the way you hold your head and shoulders—your overall stance. Your personal perception affects your choice in clothing, hairstyle, and makeup. Your view of you clearly affects your mood, which in turn affects your eating habits and your actions in every part of your day. Whew! How's that for realizing the importance of a healthy self-image? So we start where it matters most.

In this first chapter we'll focus on the inside; in the next chapter we cover the outside. Put them together, and you'll have the whole package of a magnetic woman. Watch out world, here you come!

My uncle Darwin always says "You are what you think about most of the time." Proverbs says "As [a man] thinks in his heart, so is he."[2] I say, if you stop your stinkin' thinkin' you'll become the one you were meant to be—your very best you. Everyone has personal magnetism; some of you are just allowing your magnetism to hide in a shell. If you're one of those people, then let's change things right now. You can and will master the art of first impressions by committing to take little, consistent steps to transform your own perception of you, thus improving your presentation to the world each time you walk out the door.

I must say I'm impressed with you already. You believe you can change your present dating experience, or you would not have picked up this book. I am even more impressed because not only did you buy this book, you are actually reading it, which means you are willing to take the necessary steps to get the life you want. You're not a dreamer. You're a doer! Kudos to you! Believe me, things are about to happen!

Your gumption for change reveals the fact that there is a magnetic woman in you about to emerge. Keep reading, follow these tips, and soon you will actively possess the five major qualities of the magnetic woman. You will become *courageous, confident, compelling, covert,* and *charismatic!*

For the Shy One

Every single woman dreams of walking into a room and automatically attracting the attention of that dashing bachelor. Do you have to be a vivacious, outgoing creature to attract him when the real you is comfortably quiet and introverted? No, you don't have to be someone you're not. Coy and bashful can work for you. The kicker is that the coy and bashful still has to be courageous enough to catch his eye by meeting his gaze (I'll teach you how to do this soon); otherwise, you will evaporate from his mind before an indelible impression is burned. Think Sharpie permanent marker not dry-erase pen. You have to connect no matter who you are, or you will remain unknown, unseen, or simply forgotten.

If you are extremely shy and insecure about dating, let me teach you a technique that can help you get through those scary one-on-one encounters with the opposite sex. The main work of this technique can be done when you are by yourself, all cozy in your own room. Grab a pen and something to write on. Get comfortable and think with me for a few moments.

Is there some environment where you are not shy? Are there times when you are comfortable enough to carry on an engaging conversation, times when you let loose and the real you emerges? Visualize those relaxed times with me. What are those scenarios? Ponder this and write them down. When is it safe to come out of your shell? What is your mood? How do you look? Who is around? Are you inside or outside? What are the details of a safe environment for you? Describe those scenes in detail on paper.

Now the next time you feel a "shy" coming on, bring these memories back to your mind. Breathe in all the vivid detail that you wrote about, so you can later bring them to mind when you need courage. These memories can help you relax and summon the courage to calm your pounding heart—enough courage to hold your head up and meet someone's gaze without passing out or running out the door.

You possess that magnetic power inside you, even if it is hidden far out of reach at this very moment. You just need to take a deep breath and mentally draw upon the "safe environment" you just wrote about so this side of you can emerge.

Developing an Attitude of Gratitude

Your magnetic power will begin to appear when you exchange any stinkin' thinkin' for an attitude of gratitude. Remember Bobby McFerrin's hit song "Don't Worry, Be Happy!" from the Tom Cruise movie *Cocktail*? Such a simple concept, but it's the key to a winning attitude.

Hello . . . dating is meant to be fun! No matter how many times your love life has let you down, decide from this moment on to maintain an attitude of gratitude, thankful that the bad guys are gone and the good ones are on the way. Daily life has enough worries of its own. You can't afford to hold on to negative thinking, especially about the opposite sex—not if you want to get that automatic second date. So let go of the baggage from your past. Yes, you still have to deal with your problems, but train yourself to focus on the bright side. You can find something to be grateful for in every situation—sometimes it just takes a while to see it. Even a bad breakup eventually has a positive side. You can be grateful that you are finally rid of a bad guy, even if you didn't know he was bad for you at the time.

Some of you may require more practice than others, but I urge you to make the effort to choose happiness, no matter what, because people are drawn to those with a sparkle in their eyes and repelled by those carrying a chip on their shoulders—and you cannot hide your attitude for long.

Perhaps the best description of the importance of attitude was given by the prolific author Charles Swindoll. I first saw this quote on a poster several years ago, and it has guided me ever since:

> *Attitude, to me, is more important than facts. It is more important than the past . . . than circumstances, than failure, than successes, than what other people think or say or do. It is more important than appearance, giftedness or skill. . . . We cannot change our past . . . we cannot change the fact that people will act in a certain way. We cannot change the inevitable. The only thing we can do is play on the one string we have, and that is our attitude. . . . I am convinced that life is 10% what happens to me and 90% how I react to it.*[3]

You Are What You Think About

If we are what we think about most of the time, then we need to think about what and who we want to be. Right thinking precedes and enables right actions. So . . . if you think right, you'll be able to take the actions necessary to become right. This new attitude must become a part of you. It's a matter of focusing on the good rather than the bad. If you remain focused on your painful past or creepy previous relationships, you will walk around with a chip on your shoulder that virtually everyone can see but you, scaring away dates left and right.

And unless you are still an infant, you have already experienced your share of pain and rejection. Haven't we all? Your *reaction* to rejection, not the rejection itself, has molded you into the person you are today. The more you have been hurt, the more you get shot down, the more likely you are to either steer clear of love or buy into the rejection, allowing your low view of self to affect your choices in men.

You see, you only choose men you feel are worthy of you. That is wonderful if you have a healthy perception of yourself, but damaging if you have a low view of you. If you think you are worthless, you will be drawn to bad guys and run from the good ones. You won't even know you're doing it. You'll either be repelled by nice guys, assuming they're geeks or boring, or they'll be invisible to you. And soon you'll begin to think that all men are creeps, not realizing it is your own choices that are validating that view.

People with low self-esteem are more likely to engage in behavior, or put up with behavior from others, that makes them feel bad. They do this because they feel unworthy of more. Those with high self-esteem, on the other hand, will not put up with bad behavior from others. Think about it. Do you think strippers, exotic dancers, or prostitutes have high self-esteem? Something happened to them, often in childhood, to strip them of their self-respect. Starved for affection, they take attention the only way they know how, by numbing their minds and selling their bodies.

If you have had a lot of abuse in your life, until you seek help and find healing, you are at risk of attracting another abuser. He may not look like an abuser, but eventually the abuser in him will emerge. That's not fair, but it is how it works. We are subconsciously attracted to what is "normal" for us, not what we would *like* to be normal. That is why so many women end up marrying men just like their fathers. It feels normal and thus comfortable (even if it is painful). I urge you to do the needed work on your life so you can face the sleeping giant before you marry one.

I've written an addendum at the end of this book especially for you who are struggling with your identity and worth. If you are struggling with your worthiness and value, please read it now. I offer extra tips and resources to help you get what you need to discover your true identity and personal worth. I want you to see how special you really are so you will be able to attract a date worthy of the magnetic woman hiding inside you!

It goes back to attitude, girl. Your mental position needs to be that you have but one life to live and you are going to live it to the fullest! No past hurts, present challenges, or potential rejections are going to stop you now. If life has handed you a raw deal, if your self-worth was beat down from the day you were born, it is time to turn the tide, say enough is enough, and take control. Choose the mental position that you will do what you need to do to be the magnetic person you truly are, then courageously read on, girlfriend.

Are you ready, now, to learn about the five qualities of the magnetic woman? We'll dive into the first four in this chapter and save the fifth for a chapter of its own. These five Cs will shape you into the kind of woman who attracts that first date and makes the second one *automatic*.

A Magnetic Woman Is Courageous

cour·age
Mental or moral strength to venture, persevere,
and withstand danger, fear, or difficulty[4]

I talk to single gals of all types, including the shy, the spunky, the student, the career woman, the teenager, the middle-ager, the single mom, the independent woman, the woman who's fresh on the dating circuit, and the suddenly single again.

Wherever you fall in that lineup, you can become a magnetic

woman as your answers to the following questions become yes—
even if you've still got a ways to go. Can you walk into a crowded
room and cause heads to turn your way? Do you compel others
to connect eye-to-eye when you look their way? Do you notice
people smiling back at you when you smile at them? Can you
gaze into his eyes for a few moments and turn away, then find he
has crossed the room the talk to you? Now that is a magnetic
woman! That magnetic woman can be the *real* you! I'm not talking a phony persona you don't even recognize. I'm talking the
real magnetic woman who may be currently hidden away inside
of you. In order to find that person, you must commit to adopting
a winning attitude about your own personal identity.

Feel the fear and do it anyway! It's the only way to master any
skill. Just as right thinking precedes right actions, right actions
precede right feelings. If you wait until you *feel* confident before
you try to *act* confident, you'll never get there. Push through the
fear, even if your hands are shaking and your knees are knocking.
Push through your discomfort and hold your head up. Push those
shoulders back and look that person straight in the eye. Before
you know it, you will no longer be faking confidence, you will
have achieved it!

Courage is pushing beyond the pain of your past and rising
above adversity so you can start over. The only way to conquer
fear and gain courage is to face it. So, I ask you, what is the worst
thing that can happen if you put yourself out there and show interest in a man? Write that possibility down in your journal, then
think of at least two or three positive ways you can respond to
that scenario—what can you say? Having a plan ahead of time
builds instant courage for most any situation.

And besides, the majority of what we worry about never happens! Think about that for a minute. We waste so much time
holding ourselves back in love and in life because we're afraid of

something there is a 90 percent chance won't ever happen. Now that should get you to say enough is enough! Let's face this FEAR—False Evidence Appearing Real—and get on with our lives.

My personal fear was public humiliation, and I was convinced I had good reason to be afraid. I had been publicly humiliated more than once, and I allowed those experiences to change my outward behavior, believe you me.

Exactly what do I mean by public humiliation? You know, like someone responding to your advance with a shout of, "Why are you walking next to me? I don't like you. Just leave me alone!" Mind you, that happened to me when I was twelve, so he was just a boy, but I still feel the sting today if I let myself think about it. Isn't that silly? For years, it affected the way I showed my feelings; I was always afraid I would be publicly humiliated if I had the nerve to think I was worthy of someone liking me. Hence, I was convinced that any time a boy showed interest in front of other people, he was most likely just making fun of me, like in the prom scene of *Never Been Kissed* or the horror film *Carrie*.

I remember once in high school I had a class assignment to lip-synch to an Olivia Newton-John song. I borrowed my sister's fancy dress and had her apply my makeup and do my hair. When I went to school, classmate Tim whistled at me from across the campus, along with a few football players nearby. I was horrified. I was sure they were making fun of me and totally being sarcastic. I wanted to hide. I was so insecure, I did not believe I could get noticed by boys in a positive way.

Then in college, my fears were confirmed when another popular football player asked me out. I eagerly accepted, thinking, "Cool. College sure changes things," only to have him stand me up. Ha, I had proven my point—I was unworthy of love. Or had I? That guy who stood me up was notorious for breaking hearts in high school. Why did I think he had changed just because his buddies weren't right beside him? Could it have been that I was putting myself in situations to hang with popular boys of little character, known for making fun of people to increase their own public image?

I found out in my twenties that was indeed the case. I had believed a lie and then subconsciously tried to prove that lie by gravitating toward guys who treated me the way I expected to be treated. In life and in love we get what we expect to get, because that is what we seek out. And if our expectations are low, sure, we'll get there every time—which means we'll get disappointment every time. *And* we won't be able to recognize the good guys, even when they are right in front of us, because unconsciously we feel unworthy of them.

Wow, is that deep! Let's sum this up by saying it takes courage to face your fear, see the truth, and develop a new view of you—a magnetic you who deserves to have men take notice.

A Magnetic Woman Is Confident
con·fi·dent
Certain <*confident* of success or *confident*
that conditions will improve>; having or showing
assurance and self-reliance <a *confident* manner>[5]

Desperate Housewives star Nicollette Sheridan first became a star when she was in a film called *The Sure Thing* starring opposite John Cusack, and the following year she was part of the ensemble of the nighttime soap *Knots Landing*. During the time she was represented by our talent agency, she impressed me with her effortless confidence. She'd come into our offices, usually in sweats or other casual attire, wearing little or no makeup. Nicollette seemed completely unaffected by anyone around her—not in a rude "I'm above you" way, but rather a confident "I'm comfortable in my own skin" manner. Now, of course, you can argue that she is gorgeous, so it is easy for her to be unaffected. But I tell you, this was not the case. I spent nearly eleven years as a talent agent, and almost every day I saw famous, beautiful people who were over-the-top insecure.

I agree that Nicollette Sheridan is one of the pretty people who can skip makeup and still look great, but her personal magnetism was indeed a result of her confident unaffectedness. She was just who she was and didn't care what anyone else thought. She wasn't rude; she was just comfortable with herself.

In Beverly Hills, where I spent a majority of my active single years, movie stars and models walk down the street, browse Rodeo Drive, cruise by in fancy cars, or sit by you at some trendy café. It is so common, you don't always notice them. Why am I telling you this? The rich and famous are not always recognized in Tinseltown because they are a dime a dozen. It is the magnetic ones who catch our eye. And it was their magnetism and confidence that I studied, because that is what I wanted to absorb, so that I, too, could learn to turn heads.

The models and actresses I observed were possibly farther along the magnetic scale than you are at this moment, but, you'll get there—one C at a time.

Fake It Till You Make It

I am happy to inform you that you do not have to feel confident before you look confident. *Fake it till you make it* definitely works when it comes to confidence! And standing tall is one quick and easy way to fake fabulous. Stand up straight, head held high, and you will come across as self-assured (not pompous) and thus attractive—even if your hands are sweating, your knees are knocking, and your legs are shaking.

I'm a Dr. Phil fan. But I don't agree with everything he says. One such opinion I disagree with is found in his book *Love Smart*. Dr. Phil McGraw claims, "You will not succeed in the highly competitive dating game unless you are convinced that you are absolutely fabulous. . . . You cannot fake fabulous. You have to be fabulous and know that you are fabulous!"[6]

I say, well of course you can fake fabulous! It is done every single day by people in the dating, entertainment, business, and you-name-it worlds. To get a desired result, you have to fake it when you don't feel it. Period. You fake it until you make it. The more you practice being fabulous, the sooner you will feel and truly be fabulous—remember, actions come before feelings. You start by changing your *thinking* to believe that you can become fabulous, then you *act* as if you are fabulous, until finally your *feelings* catch up with your thinking and actions, and it all comes together. Think—act—feel.

American Idol's sixth runner-up in season five, Kellie Pickler, managed to fake happiness each week as Simon Cowell, Randy Jackson, and Paula Abdul publicly annihilated her performances—in front of thirty million viewing Americans. That adorable country girl from Albemarle, North Carolina, kept her bright smile, politeness, and adorable charm throughout the competition. Oh, I'm sure she cried when she got back to her hotel room; but she faked happiness, charm, and confidence until she got there. And America? We fell in love with her for it.

So if you are terrified to look someone in the eye, pretend you are the most confident person in the world—lift up your head, assume the posture, and look that person in the eye. Feel the fear and do it anyway. With practice and a few embarrassing moments (which won't kill you), you will emerge a confident woman people are eager to be near!

As my dad always says, "Nothing worthwhile comes easy." It takes conscious effort. Work at it until you have enough small victories, and confidence will become second nature. I know I keep repeating the same thing over and over, but I'm saying it again: feelings follow actions. Remember, it's think, act, feel. If you wait to feel magnetic before you act magnetic, you will never get there. Act confident, and you will soon feel confident. It only takes one little victory of stepping out of your comfort zone to build momentum for the next time, and from there you'll be willing to risk again and again. Before you know it, you'll wonder how you ever feared looking a man in the eyes.

Demure Confidence Works Too

As I mentioned above when I was chatting with you shy gals out there, a magnetic woman is also at times demure. Quite an appealing trait. A demure girl is coy or shy.[7] A man likes a shy, coy, well-mannered lady just as much as a funny, outgoing, direct gal. Both layers are intriguing and keep him guessing. The ideal is to have all these traits wrapped up in the same woman. We all have these sides, though some are just more repressed than others because of insecurity or life experiences that have taught us to repress them.

Demure confidence from a respectable lady draws attention, especially these days when it is rather rare. Whenever I attracted a famous bad boy, I was pursued because I was demure and thus different from the usual girls in his circles. As his antithesis, I became a challenge that intrigued him. Before long he asked for my phone number. His appeal to me (aside from his fame) was my naive thought that I could change him over to my lifestyle. Neither of us won, but both sides had fun trying.

A Magnetic Woman Is Compelling
com·pel
To drive or urge forcefully or irresistibly; to cause to do or occur by overwhelming pressure[8]

A compelling woman is irresistible because she knows where she's been and what she wants, and she pursues her own destiny. Other women want to be like her, and men want to be with her. You can be her by spending time getting to know yourself and revisiting your dreams.

Have you made up your wish list for an ideal date? I am so impressed if you already have one. You're probably already compelling and didn't even know it. Pull out your list and revisit it to see if you want to update any wishes for your next first date. If you haven't written out your wish list, here's your chance. Grab your journal, and let's design your perfect mate. Imagine yourself already a fabulous, alluring, magnetic woman. Now grab your pen and describe the man who deserves that woman. What are his qualities? What does he look like? What is his job description? How important and strong is his faith? Ponder every detail you want in your next date, right down to the color of his hair.

Can you date someone who doesn't exactly match your list? Sure you can. Compelling women attract men of all shapes and sizes. You will attract and be attracted to men who don't match your list, and you'll discover that some of them have some of the important qualities on your list. Others won't have any at all. Prioritize your list for which qualities are "must haves" and which are just "nice to haves," so you can decide who gets a shot and who doesn't.

You've got to have that list if you want to choose your dates well. Why? Here's a scary reality: every one of us has this invisible GPS, a homing device magnetizing us to those who are at the same emotional level we are at. That reality alone should be your wake-up call to do all you possibly can to get emotionally healthy so you can finally attract men who are internally desirable, rather than emotional disasters.

The Unwanted and Wanted Posters

In *Finding a Man Worth Keeping*, I had you write out your want ad, based on the qualities you've been getting from your relationships thus far. If you didn't do it then, do it now. Using one piece of paper (or page in your journal) for each past relationship, at the top of the page write the ex-boyfriend's name, then draw a line down the middle of the page. List all his good qualities on one side and bad qualities on the other. Do this for every guy you've gone out with. After you're done, go back and circle every negative and positive quality that is repeated in at least two of your guys. Cross out everything else.

Now you'll need a big piece of construction paper or poster board, a pair of scissors, and some old magazines, newspapers, and catalogs. On one side of the poster board, write in bold letters at the top UNWANTED. On the reverse side of your poster board, write WANTED. Now, look at the list of circled negative qualities from previous dates. Cut out words and pictures from your magazines, newspapers, and catalogs that represent this unwanted guy and the unwanted life you've been living, then glue or tape them on the UNWANTED side. Do the same for the

WANTED side of your poster—revealing the man and the lifestyle you want. Add to the WANTED side, words and pictures of qualities you want in your ideal guy but haven't yet found. Keep this double-sided poster at home as a humorous reminder of where you've been and where you're going. It will inspire you.

Compelling Women Face Their Shortcomings

Facing our shortcomings is not always easy, but you can't fix what's broken unless you know where the break is. While you do your poster exercise, think through and write down answers to these profound questions:

1. Though different on the outside, do your dates repeatedly end up looking the same on the inside, maybe not physically or professionally, but in the way they treat you? If so, in what ways are they the same, and why do you think you are attracted to those character traits?

2. Are you getting the same results each time you meet someone new? Perhaps you get asked out on a few first dates but rarely a second. If he does call to see you again, he doesn't ask to take you on an official date; rather, he just calls at the last minute and has you come over to his place. If so, what do you think happened for him to infer that you deserve less than first-class treatment?

3. Have you gotten feedback from any of your dates, either directly or from a third party who set you up? What was said? Were there comments like you were too needy, too chatty, too whiny, too sassy, too messy, too tidy, too . . . anything? What was his "complaint," and was there any validity to his claim? If so, is that something you want to change about yourself?

Once you identify the problem, remedies are available for most any dating dilemma. If, for example, all your dates end up treating you in the same poor manner, the solution is to learn to command respect by building your self-esteem. When you feel good about who you are, you will be turned off and lose interest in anyone who treats you less than you deserve to be treated. If you find that dates usually call you at the last minute and rarely spend money on you or take you out in public, there's an easy fix for that. Stop accepting last-minute dates. Problem solved. (We'll talk about this in more detail in chapters 5 and 10.) If dates often give you the brush-off—like they're busy right now or some other excuse—you possibly have acted too needy or tried to get too serious too soon. That's fixable as well, just don't freak out your *next* first date with any talk of a future together! Let the potential future of you two be a progressive dialogue over many dates, not the first few.

I know it's not fun to reminisce on the negative, but there's a great payoff to figuring out why you got a certain negative result: you can figure out how to obtain a positive result next time. You have to know what's missing before you can add it, you have to know what's cracked to mend it, and you have to know what's wrong to make it right. Thinking about these three questions is a big step toward your desired result—that soon-to-be automatic 2nd date.

Compelling women are proactive. They look at where they've been, face their shortcomings, make necessary changes, and progressively move toward their goal.

Compelling Women Uncover Their Unique Qualities

The prince in *Ever After*—one of my all-time favorite chick flicks—was irresistibly drawn to Drew Barrymore's depiction of Cinderella, not because she was the most beautiful young maiden in town, but because she was different. She knew who she was and what she wanted. She was demure yet possessed plenty of spunk as she respectfully spoke her mind. She was also profoundly well-read, a quality found in no other women in her town.

What makes *you* intriguing? What is unique about your background, hobbies, talents, experiences, travel, jobs, languages, and knowledge? You may be surprised to find out you have done a lot of unique things and possess qualities few others have. Begin writing out your autobiography, and see what the pages of your life reveal. You might surprise yourself and discover that your life has been fascinating!

Compelling Women Are Creative

Oh, yes, you have a creative side. Your creativity may be underdeveloped, like unused muscles that crave a visit to the gym. Your creative "muscles," like your physical muscles, operate under the "use it or lose it" policy. Don't you think it's time to exercise that side of your brain? Do you like to draw, paint, sing, or write? Do you enjoy going to the movies, the theatre, the ballet, the museum, or the opera, even if it's by yourself?

Few people take advantage of the tourist attractions or nature adventures in their local cities. They get spoiled or bogged down by busy, daily lives. But no, no, no, not you. You are creative, and creative people know their towns and know what's happening around them because they've made the effort to explore. Do this, and you will not only add depth to your life, you will also meet intriguing new people in the process, and it may include your next first date.

What are your dreams, aspirations, interests, and hobbies? Stop right now to fill a page in your journal by writing them down. Then write three things you will do *this* week to pursue these interests. Each week come up with three more things, insignificant as they may seem, to move toward your worthwhile goals. Pursue this new and improved life while you are searching for your next first date, and you will inevitably become intriguing. If you spend your early dates revealing these intriguing things about yourself—rather than focusing on hardship, bitterness, or wrongs suffered—your dates will be calling you again and again.

Compelling Women Have Spunk

Do you have spunk? Do people chuckle at some of the things you say or do? Are you known to have a firm opinion on certain things and a willingness to share these views? Do you have the courage to say the one thing no one else dares to say, and yet you think of it as no big deal? All these traits are chalked up to "spunk" and are quite compelling to most any bachelor.

Don't be one who always takes the safe road and follows along with the crowd. You won't stand out that way. I love the country song that says "You've got to stand for something or you'll fall for anything." My personal faith is the most precious thing to me. Oh, I've taken a lot of ribbing for it—especially in Hollywood, where religion is cool as long as your belief is in "god," small g. This is the kind of religion where any kind of god is okay and all religions are simply variations of the same thing, so believe whatever you want and you're cool. But if you let it be known that you believe in Jesus Christ as the only true God—yikes!—you are labeled narrow-minded, judgmental, and rude. The labels may be inaccurate, but you are still left to withstand the wrath of such popular opinion, no matter how compassionately you behave. Do you have the spunk to make a defense for who you are? Or do you bend every way the wind blows? A compelling, thus magnetic, woman takes a stand no matter how hot the fire gets. And for that, you may be publicly roasted. But I tell you from personal experience: you will most definitely be privately respected and at times even publicly respected. You want to be intriguing? Stand for something.

A Magnetic Woman Is Covert

co·vert

Not openly shown, engaged in, or avowed; veiled <a *covert* alliance>[9]

Here's a little secret: a magnetic woman knows the covert game of chasing a man until he catches her! You, my dear, don't chase men; no, no, no. In fact, this is all a covert, discreet operation of drawing men to you. You let him know you are *interested*—you don't have to hide that—but it is how you let him know you're available and interested that matters. In this section, I will teach you the covert art of *flirting*.

When you flirt, you are not officially chasing the boys; rather, you are compelling them to chase you. Men want to do the chasing, because they are natural-born hunters. Sure, you are putting great effort into finding and attracting available men, but you are doing it in such a way that he is the pursuer and you are the pursuee!

Men want to be confident that you will agree to go out with them when they ask you, so you covertly give them this confidence through flirting. This allows men to make the official move with the confidence that you'll say yes, while maintaining the perception that they are in control.

Flirting actually works for you in several ways. Not only does it spare you the kind of rejections you've dealt with in the past, it does wonders for a man's ego by letting him know you're interested. You see, more than most women realize, many men are shy and insecure. It's nice for them to get some reassurance now and then. Easing fear of rejection, flirting clues the man in that it's safe to make an approach—a win for him because there's a lot of pressure on the male to make all the moves. By flirting, you are engaging in a covert operation of letting your potential date know of your interest—just to help him out—now, isn't that thoughtful?

Bottom line, flirting is a fun, nondirect way of attracting a great guy, without risking the rejection of a more direct approach. It's the easy way to get asked out by that cutie when you don't have the luxury of someone to set you up. And the *key* to flirting is appropriate, inviting eye contact.

Does Anyone Really See Me?

Our society is not personal enough these days. Lack of personal eye contact may be due to being shy, but I'm suspicious it has more to do with being preoccupied. Taking the time to look into another human's eyes can transform any relationship, at all levels of your life; it makes people feel like they are really seen, heard, and thus matter. Wow, all that from a little eye-to-eye connection. And one of the many benefits of developing a style of direct eye contact is that, when appropriate, flirting becomes automatic and effortless.

Determine from this point on to consciously and deliberately practice actually looking at people in your everyday path, both male and female. Obviously I'm not suggesting you flirt with married men or other women. I'm suggesting you make more eye-to-eye human contact, including *with* women. I'm talking about taking the risk, on a daily basis, to look people in the eye and hold their gaze for at least a second. Practice this often—anywhere or anytime. Try it at the fast-food counter, in the grocery store, dry cleaners, bank, or at church. Anytime you exchange money with a cashier, checker, or fast-food clerk, look the attendant in the eye. By the way, if your gaze is meant to be platonic, it's best to keep it under three seconds.

It may feel weird and uncomfortable the first time you look your fast-food clerk in the eye. If it does, you'll know you haven't been really seeing people around you. They take your order, accept your cash or debit card, and give you food most every day; yet you aren't seeing them really. Be different. Be compelling. When you look into someone's eye, you look into his soul.

As you grow more and more accustomed to looking strangers in the eye, it will become comfortable for you to scan a room and look that cute single guy in the eye and nonverbally communicate your interest in him.

The Art of Silent Conversation

Here is my quick description of the three-second flirt: when you cross paths with a man who intrigues you, discreetly position yourself so you are in his line of vision—be it across a crowded room, in a classroom, in a business meeting, across the street, or standing in line. Then look invitingly into his eyes. That's right, you catch his eye. When your eyes meet, offer him your full attention with a focused three-second gaze (one-one-thousand, two-one-thousand, three-one-thousand). The eyes meet; you speak with your eyes, then your mouth curves into the smile—not a huge smile, rather your best, soft, "I'm intrigued" smile. You end your three-second flirt with a smile as you casually look away.

Three seconds of gazing is plenty of time to speak volumes. If you can muster the courage to hold the gaze five seconds, you go, girl! There will be little doubt that you are interested. If you hold your gaze any longer than five seconds, however, you've just bordered on creepy. Most likely he will look away first, not a good sign. Practice makes perfect. So set out to practice flirting a little bit every day.

With the goal of mastering this three-second flirt, the next time you are out and about, make it a personal challenge to zero in on at least three apparently single men (no rings on their fingers) and practice your flirting skills.

Are you ready to find a potential date? Here's your step-by-step on how to bring him on over: Slowly scan the room with calm, soft eyes, resting your eyes briefly on any man who captures your attention, then casually glance for a bare ring finger. If his finger is bare, lock into a gaze for your three-second flirt. Again, silently count it out if you need to—*one-one-thousand, two-one-thousand, three-one-thousand*—add a slight smile or grin, and then casually look away. But remember, this isn't a see-who-blinks-first starring contest. You are merely going for getting noticed, something rather important for gaining first dates.

You are not a failure if you aren't noticed by your man the very first time you meet his gaze. If he hasn't jumped out of his seat and rushed over to meet you, wait a few minutes then re-engage his eyes a second, third, or even fourth time during the time you are in the same place at the same time. Don't assume you've blown it if you are not asked out on this first encounter. He may not have known you were available, he may be shy or temporarily unavailable, or you may need to work on your flirting skills.

Repetition is a good thing. When you think about it, it is natural to connect with someone who intrigues you either consciously or subconsciously. Haven't you ever caught yourself looking at some stranger over and over in a crowded restaurant. You don't mean to stare, so you look away a bit before you sneak another peek. I'm just teaching you how to do this to get your desired results—a conversation and maybe even a request for a date! It just takes a little practice.

Another reason it may take more than one flirtatious gaze is that he may not be sure he's reading you right. He may *think* you noticed him, but he may also think you might be confusing him for someone else. By the third or fourth pass, he'll get the picture without your coming across as obnoxious, because you're being subtle.

I hope you are catching on that the art of flirting involves more than your eyes. Your body language can also let him know you're interested. If you stand with your arms uncrossed, you'll convey that you are *open*, and when you maintain great posture—shoulders back, head held up, and stomach pulled in tight—you'll communicate that you are *confident*.

It's Like We've Known Each Other for Years

Think of flirting as developing a nonverbal conversation. Things are happening around you that both you and your potential date may notice. When something merits a reaction, you can look his way with a "knowing look." You are trying to get on his same wavelength, reacting to your shared environment and hoping to create a bond between you two. Say you saw something cute, like a child doing something adorable or an elderly couple being sweet and romantic. Look his way and smile to get across, "Wasn't that cute." If a waiter drops a tray of food, you can look his way and chuckle, raise an eyebrow, or express a nonverbal "oops." If conflict arises around one of you, you can look at each other to communicate, "Oh no, what's going to happen next?" If the entire event you have both found yourselves attending is totally boring, you can look at him for shared sympathy. Develop a conversation through flirting, without saying a word, and he will feel like he's known you forever. It will be natural for him to come over and chat with his "old friend."

Covertly practice these skills, and you will reveal your interest in a safe, nonconfrontational manner. If flirting does not cause this man to come over and get your number, no need to feel rejected, because you did not exchange words. You merely engaged in a covert operation. The secret is safe with you. Keep being magnetic, and keep practicing wherever you encounter enticing single men. Sooner than you think, all these techniques will click, and men will automatically begin making moves to strike up conversations with *you*.

Automatic Recap

1. Magnetic women make great first impressions.
   - First impressions happen in moments—before you ever open your mouth.
   - People judge you by your posture, expressions, gestures, hairstyle, clothes, physique, and beauty.
   - Your impression of you affects every part of your outward presentation.
   - Coy and bashful can attract as well as vivacious and outgoing, as long as you muster up the courage to look that man in the eye and hold his gaze for a moment before you smile and turn away.
2. Magnetic women have great attitudes.
   - How you *think* about yourself determines how you *act*, and how you act determines how you

feel, and all of this affects the life and love you find.

- Magnetic women have a positive mental outlook about themselves and their appeal to the opposite sex.

- Changing your attitude changes your vibe (that unconscious, nonverbal message your very presence emits), which changes your response from men.

- Since we only choose men we feel worthy of, you owe it to yourself to work on your perception of yourself until you believe you're worthy of quality, treat-you-right men.

3. Magnetic women have courage.

- Courage is the mental strength to withstand rejection and the mental tenacity to pursue the real fabulous woman inside.

- To gain courage, face your fear and step out of your comfort zone. The worst that can happen is rejection, and you've already been there, done that, and survived.

4. Magnetic women exude confidence.

- Confidence shows through in your self-assurance and self-reliance.

- You can look confident before you feel confident—just fake it till you make it.

- Confident women are at times demure—coy, using modest, playful flirtation. Men love demure, well-mannered ladies just as much as funny, outgoing gals.

5. Magnetic women are compelling.

- Knowing what you want is easy when you grab a

pen and write out your starry-eyed wish list for the man of your dreams.

- Compelling women face their shortcomings and are dedicated to improving themselves.
- Compelling women are different, creative, and not afraid to show their spunk.

6. Magnetic women are covert.

- Covert women know how to pursue a man so discreetly that he thinks he is the one making the pursuit! She chases him until he catches her!
- Magnetic women confidently master the three-second flirt and practice it daily until it is an automatic part of their single lives.
- Covert women love to flirt, anytime, anywhere, just by looking any appealing single man right in the eye. Look up, scan the room, zero in, and make contact.

The Magnetic Woman Emerges

I am so excited for you right now, I am bursting at the seams. You have found the courage to step out of your comfort zone, feel the fear, and adopt a winning attitude! You now know that you can show yourself to be confident even if you have to fake it till you feel it. You've discovered that you are a compelling woman who knows where she's been, what she wants, and where she's going. And you've learned how to look the world in the eye and flirt across a crowded room. I would say that is huge, wouldn't you?

All that's left to develop in your magnetic personality is your charisma. Turn to the next chapter and let's find your beauty in the eye of the beholder.

Automatic Journaling
Making Magnetic Happen

1. With your new "don't worry, be happy" attitude, list ten things about yourself or your present life you are thankful for right now.
2. Let's explore the possibility that some of your negative views about men are false.
   a. Write down one negative assumption you have about men along with the name of some guys from your past who have confirmed this belief.
   b. Now, write down the opposing viewpoint and read it out loud to hear yourself say it.
   c. Write down one thing about your behavior toward men that would change if you believed the opposite of your negative view of men.
3. Go someplace where there are people you don't yet know, and make direct eye contact with three strangers; then smile at them before you look away. Write down how it felt. Was it comfortable, odd, nerve wracking, fun, terrifying?
4. Today is the day to be daring and bold. The day to feel the fear and do it anyway. The day to fake it till you make it. So write down a few things you have been putting off due to fear of failure—anything from speaking in front of people to singing karaoke, riding a bike, or asking for a raise. Now, visualize yourself succeeding and taking the first step toward your goal. Now hold your head up and go out and do it. Then write down all that transpired from your courage to fake it till you make it.
5. Describe in detail a man who deserves the magnetic woman

you are becoming. Is this an easy exercise for you, or are you arguing with yourself about your personal magnetism?

6. If you haven't already made your WANTED/UNWANTED poster (I prefer the thick presentation boards so it's not flimsy) go back to page 17 and make it now. Keep it in plain view so it catches your eye often.

Revisit page 18 and thoroughly answer the three questions about facing your shortcomings:

7. Look at the list of repeated qualities from your previous relationships. Why do you think you are attracting men with these qualities?

8. Write down three less-than-favorable responses to your first dates—i.e. no second date, last-minute call for second date, or just a "come on over to my place" second get-together.

9. Thinking back to your first date, what do you think you did or said to give that man the impression you would accept that treatment?

10. Get out there and flirt. Make a chart in your journal and log in each time you flirt. How many guys did you flirt with? How many seconds did you hold his gaze? Did he look away first? Did you manage to develop a nonverbal conversation? Did he walk on over and introduce himself? How did you feel about the whole process?

The Eye of the Beholder

Presenting Your Best Outer Self

L ike much of America, I've fallen in love with Betty
Suarez, the main character on ABC's hit TV show *Ugly
Betty*. She is quite the intriguing and complex individual.
On the inside, she is a dynamic, intelligent, and talented woman;
but on the outside, she's a head-gear, braces-wearing, fashion-
challenged girl. Perhaps her outer appearance would not be as
traumatic for her if she were in a normal world, but Betty works
at the nation's top fashion magazine, and she's surrounded by superficial, ambitious snobs who trample her on a daily basis. Not
exactly the easiest place to build confidence. With each new episode, despite the challenge of her environment, we see Betty
willfully emerging more and more into a full-fledged magnetic
woman.

A Magnetic Woman Has Charisma

cha·ris·ma

Special magnetic charm or appeal; personal magic of leadership arousing special popular loyalty or enthusiasm[1]

Okay, okay, so you've learned how to summon the inner, fabulous, magnetic you. You are now courageous, confident, compelling, and covert. But you still haven't been mistaken for a supermodel. Truth be told, you feel a little like you're starring in your own version of *Ugly Betty*. What's up with that? Here you are all filled with substance and character—so why aren't the men falling head over heels for you?

Time for the question many of you have been dying to ask: can less-than-knockout-beautiful women have the magnetic power to attract men? Or does charisma—that final C in our equation of the fully empowered magnetic woman—mean you have to be physically perfect and outwardly beautiful?

I can waste your time and sugarcoat it for you, but that wouldn't be giving you your money's worth for buying this book. You've picked up this book because you want to know exactly how to attract dates and then callbacks for more dates. To do that, I have to tell you the truth, as harsh as it is, so you, yes *you*, can indeed achieve that exact goal. So here it goes: the honest, bottom-line truth is that looks do indeed play a role in attraction. It is human nature to be drawn to people we find attractive and to steer away from those we don't find "easy on the eyes." Unfair, but it is what it is.

An Experiment in Beautiful

Inspired by *Ugly Betty*, in November of 2006, TV's *Entertainment Tonight* decided to do their own experiment to find out if the general public really does discriminate according to looks. They chose as their guinea pig former cohost of MTV's *Total Request Live* Vanessa Minnillo and followed her with five hidden cameras. She played two characters. First, she was "Ugly Joy." Ugly Joy was Vanessa after a six-hour makeup transformation, including a "fat suit" to make her appear out-of-shape and frumpy, complete with braces and stringy black hair. The second character was her as the blonde bombshell "Beautiful Joy." The crew went to various locations, including a college campus, where she asked questions of those passing by. Not one guy stopped to chat to Ugly Joy, but all the ladies did. Every guy stopped to answer Beautiful Joy's questions, but none of the gals did. Hmmm . . . interesting. Later she tried to get into the hippest night spot in town. Ugly Joy could not beg her way in. Beautiful Joy was ushered in within moments.

Nancy Etcoff, a Harvard psychologist and author of *Survival of the Prettiest*,[2] found overwhelming evidence that pretty people do receive favoritism, even in unexpected areas. "We find that even in courts of law, better-looking people are given more leniencies," Etcoff says. "They're not picked up as readily for shoplifting. They're not as often convicted of a crime."[3] So, do looks matter? Well, let's be honest. Yes, they do. We can argue with this, or we can accept the reality that human nature responds more to attractive folks. But what is it that makes a woman attractive? Does she have to have flawless skin and Barbie-doll features to be beautiful?

In one of Nancy Etcoff's studies, she asked women from ten

different countries what they define as beautiful. "One of the most surprising things that we discovered was that, around the world, only two percent of women felt comfortable describing themselves as beautiful, while 98 percent of women did not." Etcoff says, "[But] when we asked women, 'What does beauty mean?' . . . They were thinking of physical attributes, they were comparing themselves to supermodels, they were saying, 'I'm not tall, I'm not thin, I'm not blonde, I don't look like the stereotype out there.' "[4]

In evaluating her experience as Ugly Joy, Vanessa Minnillo said, "We form opinions about people based on their looks, snap judgments we make within seconds of meeting someone." She added, "It's cliché to say, but if you judge every book by its cover, you'll never actually read anything."[5]

Entertainment Tonight's little "Ugly Joy" experiment was probably not a huge news flash to you. I think we've all learned from personal experience that the pretty people don't have to work as hard to gain attention from men as the less than pretty do. People notice the outside first. Our job here is to find the pretty in you. If you want to get first and second dates, you have got to care about your physical appearance; that's just the honest truth. You can ignore it and sit at home resenting the unfairness of this world and remain dateless (which is no fun). Or you can do something about it by becoming your most attractive self and begin enjoying some of the benefits society automatically lavishes on the pretty people.

If beauty is in the eye of the beholder, then you are about to behold your own outer beauty! The purpose of this chapter is to help you honestly assess your assets and your liabilities, so that you can maximize your beauty and minimize your beast (and we all have a little or a lot of both).

Who Is That Face in the Mirror?

Get ready to step in front of that mirror, take an honest look at your reflection, and think about who that person is you see in the mirror. It is vital that you consciously think about your personal perception of your outward beauty because that inward perception of yourself directly affects your outward presentation to others whether you want it to or not. So, go ahead, stop reading for five minutes and look at yourself in that mirror . . .

No, really. Right now. I'm not going anywhere. I'll wait right here for you to come back. So go on, find a mirror, full length is ideal, but if a face mirror is all you've got at this very moment, that will do for your first look.

Did you do it? Did you look in the mirror and breathe in your immediate thoughts about what you saw? What was your interpretation of your physical beauty? Wait, before you report back that you are utterly hopeless and don't like anything you see, let me encourage you a little bit here. No one is really ever totally satisfied with herself. Even supermodels pick themselves apart every time they look in the mirror.

When I was a brand-new talent agent, I was shocked at some of the comments I'd get from actors and actresses when they showed me their book of photos. They would critique what looked like physical perfection to me and say silly things like, "Now as you see in this picture, I know how to pose to hide this awfully crooked nose; so don't let that scare you away."

Whether we're "fat" or "skinny," it seems to be human nature to zero in on our own flaws—flaws sometimes invisible to others yet obsessed on by us. Even yesterday I was at the gym and met this attractive, obviously fit, petite forty-year-old woman. We started chatting about an upcoming vacation to the Bahamas and her comments were, "I don't know what I'm going to do. I'm not about to get into a bikini with *this* body, I've never been so out of shape." And you know what? She was serious. To her, she thought she was flabby and disgusting to look at. My, my, how many times have we told ourselves *When I get to this weight or this shape then I'll be happy*. And when we get there, we *still* think we're fat and we're still not satisfied. I've also been guilty of those thoughts, silly as they are. We are more critical of ourselves than anyone else is.

Ugly Betty's star, America Ferrera, and actress/Grammy Award–winning singer Queen Latifah are two magnetic women who have the body-image equation down pat—it's feeling good about yourself that gives you charisma!

"Whether you're skinny or not, there's just way too much attention placed on the way we look," said America Ferrera in a recent interview. "It overshadows more important things in life like loving yourself, loving who you are and finding yourself on the inside." Ferrera goes on to say "We're not all a size 2 and we're not all a size 0, and you know what? That's okay! . . . For me, it's about feeling good about who you are."[6]

Queen Latifah says, "There are too many people with gorgeous bodies and no self-confidence. I don't care what size you are. Confidence is sexiness to me."[7]

How do you find that charisma and that attractive self? How do you transform yourself from a passed-over plain Jane to a stop-'em-in-their-tracks lady? You start by taking an honest look in the mirror, taking inventory, and assessing what to do from there. Even if today you find yourself to be like Ugly Betty or Ugly Joy—a plain Jane in the midst of a world full of supermodels—realize that you most definitely have the potential to become a charismatic, attractive female—a magnetic woman eligible men will just love to be near.

Okay, so going right back to that mirror, look at yourself right now, just as you are this very minute. What do you see? What do you like just the way it is? What needs to change right away? Is there hidden beauty that can be brought out with a little make-over? No one else is around, so you can be honest. Where are you on your own beauty scale? What do you like and what do you dislike?

Can a change of clothing improve how you look and feel? What message is being sent with that hairstyle? Could it use a little update? Was the last time you changed it . . . back in high school? What about your face? As you look in that mirror, do you see deep lines on your forehead? Do you have a permanent scowl etched on your face? How is your smile? How expressive are your eyes? I'm just trying to get you to consciously do what everyone else regularly does within seconds of seeing us—analyze what you see.

On an overall basis are you pleased with that reflection? What part of your appearance is great just as it is? What can you improve with a little tender, loving care, and what would you like to all-out change?

With those personal impressions fresh on your mind, I'm going to share some simple ways to improve your appearance on even the tightest budget without any major time commitment. First, we'll look at three get-pretty-quick tips; second, I'll reveal simple makeup tricks; third, I offer some advice about personal style; and fourth, we'll have a little chat about our favorite topic—diet and exercise (laugh out loud).

Three Get-Pretty-Quick Tips

Here are three things you can do *right now* to transform yourself and improve your appearance. It's as easy as one, two, three: stay clean, show off your pearly whites, and stand tall. You will be amazed at how simple it is to stand out from the crowd, in a good way, if you'll just take the time to make these three suggestions lifetime habits to care about yourself and how you come across to others. Do this, and you will find yourself attracting more and more positive attention from the world around you.

A Sprinkle a Day

A no-brainer should be to pursue cleanliness and skip sloppiness. A daily splash of water and dab of deodorant can do wonders to reveal your hidden beauty and improve your appeal to men. You can bypass negative first impressions and thus increase your first dates by simply starting your day with a shower. And frankly, being dirty and sloppy is a turnoff to most people—not only to the men you are trying to attract.

Those Pearly Whites

After you have started your day with a sprinkle, light up the room with your smile! This is a great way to stand out from the crowd, and it takes no preparation. It can be done at any time of day or night. We are not talking about just any smile. Not a smirk or a halfhearted grin. Rather a fully engaged, eye-brightening, cheek-raising, lip-curving, teeth-exposing smile. A genuine smile can literally light up the room. Your smile is the warmest, friendliest part of your physical appearance. That expression tells others you are interested in them.

Walking on Air

Remember that scene in *Titanic* when Leonardo DiCaprio's character stands at the front of the boat and shouts, "I'm king of the world"? Do you remember his posture at the time? He stood up tall, reached up his arms, and spread them out in an arms-wide-open stance. You could feel the energized exuberance and confidence oozing out of his pores across the movie screen. What does your posture shout? I'm not necessarily recommending the "king of the world" position, but do begin taking notice of your own posture, stance, and walk, and think about what message you're sending.

Ever notice how confident women walk? Start noticing confident ladies wherever you go. Pick them out on TV and on the big screen. How do they carry themselves? What makes them stand out? A magnetic woman walks with her head held high, eyes looking straight ahead (not above or below people), shoulders pulled back, and her stomach pulled in tight.

Here's a little trick I learned from a personal trainer. He taught me the habit of consciously pulling my belly button inward, as though I'm trying to touch my spine with it. It strengthens your core stomach muscles, helps prevent back pain, and improves your posture all at the same time. Presto, perfect posture with little more effort than conscious thought. Cool, huh?

Your stance reveals much about what you believe about your personal beauty. If you feel unattractive, your body language may confirm that feeling: slouching shoulders and looking downward can communicate a desire to be left alone or to shut oneself off from others. But if you feel beautiful, you will exude beauty, from your posture to your smile to your overall presence. So if you don't feel pretty just yet, fake it till you make it—stand tall!

A Little Help from the Makeup Counter

Even if you don't have the face of an angel, you can enhance the face you were given with a little help from the makeup counter. Heavy, thick makeup is not the ticket here. You want to enhance what you've been given, not cover it up and change it.

To be perfectly honest, I've never been one to spend an hour in the morning getting ready. I just get too distracted. I always have. I don't know if it's because I have an undiagnosed case of attention deficit disorder (strong possibility) or because I am too insecure about the whole makeup-application process. But I do care about my looks, and I do "put my face on" before I see the world each day. But if you are willing to dedicate more time, I'm sure it will pay off. That's just not me. I don't find it practical, and besides, I don't have a canvas worth staring at for that long a period of time.

Artists who have that special knack for painting their faces are usually the same gals who have matching shoes, lipstick, purse, jewelry, and accessories. Nothing on their bodies is by accident, and they look fabulous. Decide if that is practical for you. If it is, great—go for it, you'll really stand out. But don't feel bad if you don't have it in you to spend that much time in the mirror.

For those nonartists out there, I'm going to share a few tips to help you figure out how to look good within minutes so you can get on with your day by simply accentuating your strong points.

The Basics

If you have light, thin eyelashes like me, use black mascara (I love Maybelline's Great Lash; it's inexpensive and works great). If you've got invisible eyebrows, use an eyebrow pencil. If your eyes are your best feature, play them up. It you've got great lips, focus on them. Accentuate your assets. In the very least, lip gloss, powder, and mascara makes any gal look fresh and not overdone. Three things I watch for throughout my day are a shiny nose, faded lipstick, and streaks of mascara under my eyes. They seem like small things, but I project a different persona when I stay on top of my touch-ups versus being lazy and letting them slip my mind. If you feel insecure and clueless about the whole makeup thing, go to any department store's makeup counter and ask for a free makeover. They will gladly teach you how to apply makeup in hopes you'll love their products.

My Breakthrough Lipstick Trick

Here's a tip I learned along the way that any lipstick-wearing female can benefit from. You know how sometimes you get embarrassed to find you've had lipstick on your teeth for who knows how long? You can prevent this by applying your lipstick as usual, then slipping your first finger in your mouth and popping it out slowly. This little trick catches the extra lipstick that got caught on the bottom of your lips (which means it was headed straight to your teeth!). Follow this up with a quick swipe of both the top and bottom front teeth and wham, bam, thank you ma'am, no more lipstick teeth! Turn this into a habit every time you apply color to your lips.

A Little Ray of Sunshine

If you happen to be as ivory-white skinned as this author, you will do well to find a nice self-tanner or bronzer to add a little color to your skin. My personal favorite is Coppertone Endless Summer Sunless Tanning lotion, which is about ten dollars a bottle. However, there are many others available for more or less. Try various brands of self-tanners and bronzers to see which one works best for your skin. I caution you, however, to please take my advice and make sure you read the label and definitely wash your hands afterward, or you will have freaky stained palms for a week.

The Charisma of Personal Style

Angelina Jolie is an extreme example revealing that any woman can go from raunchy to respected by a makeover of personal style. Paris Hilton, Madonna, Christina Aguilera, and Courtney Love are other celebrities who have gone back and forth from raunchy and wild to demure and sophisticated. And you know what? Their presence is more compelling, charismatic, and commanding when they go for the cleaned-up, sophisticated look. Oh, they get plenty of attention with their raunchy antics, but they do not get respect. It's little wonder that they are more favorably reviewed and accepted when they choose the classier image.

A charismatic woman has her own personal sense of style, a style that emerges from confidence rather than a style screaming for attention sprung from insecurity. Have you ever caught yourself sorting through outfits on a clothes rack at the mall, saying, "This looks just like Teri, and oh, that one looks like Kelly . . . and doesn't that look like Mom?" People have a sense of style about them. What is your style, and do you like it? Is it individual, appealing, and memorable or just a hodgepodge of clothing? If Angelina, Madonna, and Paris can change their image one outfit at a time, so can you.

Finding your own personal style is not rocket science. It's just about finding clothes that reflect who you are and what you like to do. But it's also about making the most of how you feel about what you've got and avoiding a few fashion pitfalls. Here's a few stylin' tips to help you find your own charismatic you.

A Style for Every Season

The Bible's book of Ecclesiastes reminds us that there is a time and season for everything[8], and that includes our dress code. You can fill your wardrobe for various roles you will play throughout the seasons. You may enjoy being the country girl, business woman, elegant socialite, sports star, or stunning princess. It really depends on where you are going, what you are doing, and how you view yourself. At times you may go for adorable tomboy, outdoors girl, or cheerleader. Hey, I love my jeans and tank tops in the summer. And guys love a gal sporting a team jersey, as long as it's for their favorite team.

Fill your wardrobe with clothes that reflect your own magnetic personality while fitting the scenes you'll be entering. Oh, and just as there's a time for the tomboy, there is a time for hip and trendy. But just because you dress trendy doesn't mean you have to choose sleazy fashion. Sleaze attracts sleaze. I TiVo'd the reality TV show *The Real Housewives of Orange County* on Bravo because one of my high-school classmates was on the show. On one episode one of the housewives' ex-husband held a photo shoot, taking provocative pictures of his daughter and other young models to promote his beverage company. During the shoot the TV cameras caught this dad making comments like "Ooh, she's hot, nice, sexy," and so on. Yek. It was rather creepy. If you choose clothes that complement rather than contradict your values, you'll attract men you are proud to attract, rather than get drooled on by men you should be running from.

Keep Shopping

As you're shopping for that style that makes you, you—comfort cannot be the *only* thing you look for. If those jeans make you look frumpy and overweight, then it just doesn't matter how comfortable they feel—don't buy them. Keep shopping until you find something comfortable *and* good looking. There are just too many fashion options these days to use the excuse that it's all you could find. You can camouflage most any body flaw, so take the time to choose clothes that make you look and feel good. Remember, it's not so much what you wear as long as it's stylish and looks good on your body.

Watch That Rear View

Make sure you know what your rear view is in every outfit you put on. When you shop, use the three-way mirrors in the dressing room to see that outfit from every angle. When you're home mixing and matching clothes, you may need to use a hand mirror to catch the rear view. What looks great from the front may not be as flattering from behind. So do yourself a favor and check out both views.

Matters of Your Size and Heart Rate

Unfortunately, we can't have a chapter on our personal appearance and ignore how we feel about our current size and weight. Reality is that at any given moment throughout our daily lives, our mood is affected by how we feel about how we look. Don't you just hate that? I mean, honestly, who actually looks gorgeous nonstop, every waking moment? Not even gorgeous movie stars.

And what makes it awful is that when our personal body image is negative, we tend to punish ourselves by overeating or choosing to be sedentary rather than grabbing some grapes before heading out to work off the mood swing by elevating our heart rate with some cardio.

What's a woman to do? Make a plan, that's what you do, simple as that. Write out a plan with specific goals and compelling personal reasons for healthy eating and fitness, and commit to follow it consistently, not perfectly but consistently, and celebrate each goal you achieve as you add new goals for your health, fitness, and personal appearance.

As mentioned in the last chapter, your own view of you directly impacts how the world receives you. Your mood affects your outward appearance by influencing what you eat, how you stand, how you dress, and even how you put on your makeup. One of the keys to changing unwanted moods and low self-esteem is adapting a healthy lifestyle of diet and exercise. Remember our formula of "think, act, feel"? This works for motivating us to keep pursuing worthwhile fitness goals as well. We *think* about our personal best size and fitness level and make a plan. We *act* by putting our written plan for healthier eating and exercise into motion. Then we *feel* more confident and self-assured, and, bingo, we receive more attention from the world around us.

Finding *Your* Perfect Size

Whether you have ten pounds or one hundred pounds to lose, the key to lasting change is small, consistent steps toward your goal. There is no "perfect" size, contrary to what is seen on the covers of fashion magazines and tabloids. The size you should strive for is a size that leaves you healthy and feeling good about yourself. And it's always a good idea to ask your doctor about your diet and fitness goals.

With the recent backlash against unhealthy, skinny models and news of frequent cases of anorexic and bulimic celebrities both on and off the fashion runway, it is clearer than ever that skinny does not guarantee a healthy self-esteem or any level of happiness. Would I like to be back in my size 2? Yes and no. You see, to maintain my size 2 frame, I didn't get to eat as much as I get to eat maintaining my current size, and I rather like food. So there, I am happy being a 2 no more.

What size is the right size for gaining a certain bachelor's attention? Beauty is more than dress size. Eat healthy to achieve and maintain a weight that allows you, the eye of the beholder, to feel healthy and happy inside and out. Make *that* your ideal weight and dress size—be it size 2, 4, 6, or even 10, 12, or 14). It will be just the right size for your magnetic woman inside and just the right size for your automatic second date! Because when you feel good, you look good; and your charismatic vibe will draw that man right on over.

We Are What We Eat

Most diets work for the short term, but what makes a lasting difference in your life is your long-term eating habits. How often do we hear about a woman who heroically reached a goal of losing one hundred pounds only to gain it back a year later? Is it impossible to keep weight off? No. But what happens too often is that when we're on an extended diet, we get burned out and yearn to go back to "regular eating." For lasting results, we've got to make a plan that we can live with for the rest of our lives, with ongoing new goals to keep us motivated.

Since I turned twenty I have been on most every diet written, some with better results than others. My personal favorite eating programs are Weight Watchers (www.weightwatchers .com) and Body-for-Life (www.bodyforlife.com). There are plenty of others, of course, but I personally like these because they allow for balanced eating of all your favorite foods. I am a carbohydrates lover and always will be, so the Atkins and South Beach diets clearly didn't work long-term for me. I just don't have a desire to give up pasta or bread for the rest of my life, thank you very much. I have, however, learned to love whole grains and healthy carbs, so my short stints on Atkins and South Beach hold definite residual benefits for me.

10 Easy Steps to Adapt to Your Lifestyle

1. Do eat something for breakfast (before 10 a.m.) every day to speed up your metabolism. (Skipping breakfast is *not* a good weight-loss plan. It teaches your body to store rather than eliminate food in order to sustain you in this "starvation" mode, and you'll retain or gain rather than lose.)
2. Do drink at least eight glasses of water a day.
3. Do move your body at least twenty minutes a day.
4. Do cut out fried foods at least two meals a day, if not all together.
5. Do eat fruits and vegetables at least twice a day.
6. Do keep motivated by reading fitness and health books and magazines and visiting their Web sites.
7. Do celebrate when you achieve each little victory, be it losing five pounds or sticking with a program for three weeks. Write down your accomplishments and do something just for you.

8. Don't eat after 8 p.m.
9. Don't step on a scale more than once a week (and realize that once a month you carry about three to five pounds of water weight).
10. Don't quit if you cheat or mess up on your eating or fitness plan. Just keep going without skipping a beat. You're not striving for perfection; you're striving for a healthy lifestyle.

You've Got to Move It, Move It, Move It!

Exercise—ugh, that four-letter word I hate (you know—p-a-i-n). I've just never really enjoyed working out. I do it because I have to. And when I don't, I pay the price of being out of shape and cranky about it. Without a *plan, written goals,* and *measurable results,* I just don't stay faithful. What about you? What can you do to move your body at least twenty minutes a day? This can be blatant exercise like jogging, running, hiking, aerobics, or sports. But it can also be strapping on a pedometer and finding ways to take more steps throughout your day, such as parking a distance from the store's entrance, taking the stairs instead of the elevator, making three trips to your room with the laundry, or walking around your neighborhood, office, or school.

Seek out ways to keep going when your scale is not your friend. Find a girlfriend to buddy up with as a workout partner. Join a nearby gym. Try Jazzercize. Listen to motivational CDs while you work out. Try yoga or Pilates. There are endless options. Read everything you can get your hands on, and design an exciting fitness plan you can follow. Some of my favorite magazines are *First for Women, Fitness, Prevention, Shape,* and *Weight Watchers.* Just make a plan, make it exciting, and stick with it.

You *Can* Do This

Trust me. You can do this. No matter how many times you've failed in the past, you can start over today and strive for the ideal you! Jump-start, then keep up, your motivation by writing down all you eat, how much you move, and each goal you achieve. Celebrate each victory along the way, no matter how small. Every new "win" will cheer you on and energize you to keep going. There is no perfect size. But there is a healthy size for each of us. With the help of your doctor, find out what that is, and love yourself enough to pursue it consistently. The need for ongoing motivation will always be there. Write down your goals and enjoy the benefits of a new view of you.

Revisit That Reflection

Okay ladies, it's time to take another look in that mirror. If you've given your appearance the TLC it deserves, (1) you've taken care of the basics (keeping clean, smiling brightly, and standing up straight); (2) you're staying on top of your makeup needs; (3) you're developing your own personal style; and (4) you've made a healthy eating and exercise plan. Now it's time to revisit that full-length mirror and check yourself out for progress.

Is there already noticeable positive change in what you see? Do you see your magnetic self shining through your reflection? I am going to take for granted that you are proud of the improvements you've made thus far, no matter how small. I am proud of you as well. Isn't it exciting to see what a little extra time and focus can do? And hey, it only takes twenty-one days to form a habit, so if you incorporate these basics into your routine every day for three weeks, you'll be living your new plan, hardly thinking about it!

If you find that a part of your physical appearance is still bugging you, even after taking these four charismatic self-improvement steps we've covered thus far in this chapter, there are a few more options we can discuss. You might consider procedures as simple as waxing to something more drastic like plastic surgery. If you are thinking of the latter, make sure you are considering it because *you* want it and not because you feel pressure from family and friends.

Wax Here, Tweeze There

Inexpensive and relatively painless improvements in your appearance can reap huge rewards in your self-esteem and popularity. You can start with something as simple as tweezing or plucking your eyebrows or any unwanted facial or chin hairs. Or you can get a professional to help you out by waxing your eyebrows, legs, underarms, or facial hair. Laser hair removal is more and more popular these days, but it is also more expensive than waxing or tweezing. The upside to a laser procedure is that it is permanent. Do it once and forget about it.

Brighten That Smile

Has frequent caffeine intake caused your teeth to yellow? Check into whitening your teeth. As new whitening methods come out, the process becomes more and more affordable. You can try an over-the-counter whitener or go to your dentist for the whitening trays or one-time bleaching treatment. Call your dentist for a price quote.

If your teeth are an insecure subject for you, perhaps you can check out the latest in the orthodontist and cosmetic dentistry world. They even have clear and colored braces these days in addition to the standard silver. Veneers are more common as well. Check out your options to see if a new smile would improve your self-esteem and give you the confidence to show those pearly whites.

Get Rid of Pesky Growths

Do you have pesky, unsightly moles, growths, or warts? Have your doctor check them out and ask about having them removed. Insurance usually pays for most growth removals, so it should cost you little to nothing and end up taking away a needless source of insecurity and self-consciousness.

Dare You Go Further?

These days cosmetic enhancements are so common you would be surprised which of your friends have had a little improvement done during a recent day off. And procedures are more and more noninvasive. Even the ol' traditional nose job has alternatives these days. Cutting-edge options seem to emerge on the market every year.

A recent *Entertainment Tonight* reported that more and more people, not only stars, are choosing nonsurgical procedures to improve their appearance rather than going under the knife. In a recent study 81 percent of the more than eleven million annual cosmetic procedures were nonsurgical. The latest in the field is injectable fillers like Botox, Sculptra, and Juvéderm. These are touted as simple, noninvasive procedures that can make you look years younger. Another option is targeted lasers, which supposedly feel like little rubber-band snaps. They erase brown spots, pesky red vessels, acne scars, and wrinkles.

"More people are realizing that it's never been simpler, it's never been safer, it's never been easier to look better, that you don't have to get surgery [and] that you can get a five-minute office procedure," says Dr. Rebecca Fitzgerald, a dermatologist in Los Angeles who offers nonsurgical procedures. Dr. Fitzgerald says that there are several ways to turn back time, including Botox. But what's really moving in on facelifts are injectable fillers that are used to pump up and plump up your skin. "You don't risk as much, because you're not getting surgery, [there's] not as much downtime, you don't have to take as much time off from work, [and you're] not swollen or bruised," says Dr. Fitzgerald. "And these are very affordable procedures."[9] For more information on Dr. Fitzgerald's facial rejuvenation procedures, check out her Web site at www.rebeccafitzgeraldmd.com.

Two official Web sites worth checking out to research the latest in any cosmetic fixes as well as research doctors are www.plasticsurgery.com and www.cosmeticsurgery.com. These sites explain procedures, recovery, expected results, and prices. Since the arrival of Google, research is quicker and easier than ever. Just type in a few keywords of what you're thinking about having done (tummy tuck, nose job, face lift, chemical peel, etc.).

No form of medical procedure should be done frivolously, be it surgery, lunchtime procedures, or injectable fillers. Get referrals. Check out your doctor. Read everything you can on the various types of procedures available for any desired result. Learn the risks, the pain, the recovery, and costs involved. Most important, make sure you are doing it for yourself and not for someone else.

It's Amazing What a Little Attention Will Do

A little attention to our exterior will do wonders on your magnetism quotient, and the confidence boost will help your inner beauty as well. Did you see the series of makeovers on *Oprah* a while back? She had her producers go out on the streets and find some guys and gals who were unkempt, lost in another decade, or just in need of some serious attention. The makeover included one new outfit, a new hairstyle, and makeup application. That was all. The contestants were almost unrecognizable when it was done—they seemed to walk taller and with more confidence because they beheld their own personal beauty and liked what they saw.

Do you want to just dream about an *Oprah* makeover, or are you willing to take the initiative to invest in yourself so you can become the best you can be? If you weren't born drop-dead gorgeous, be thankful you were given the opportunity to develop character first. How's that for a new perspective?

Make the effort. Take the time to create a makeover plan and commit to improving and maintaining your outer beauty, just as passionately as you commit to continually working on your inner beauty. The steps to your own personal improvement may be one or many. Your plans can be as simple as a hairstyle change or as complex as plastic surgery. Whatever you decide to do, the only one who can change you is you!

And speaking of makeovers, remember the show *Extreme Makeover*? Those clients received major cosmetic surgery, dental work, and personal training to achieve their life-altering transformations. Most people don't require that much. When that show was on the air, I happened to be at the mall with my kids during one of their open casting calls. There were hundreds, no thousands, surrounding that mall looking for a chance at free plastic surgery.

The crowd intrigued me, so I casually walked the line to observe those wannabe contestants. Only a few were chosen, and those were individuals with severe and obvious physical needs. Most of the people in the line, however, looked like people you walk by every day. I mean absolutely normal, fine-looking people who apparently thought they were in need of a transformation. What most of them needed was a little personal makeover of the nonsurgery kind discussed earlier, such as an updated hairstyle, a new outfit, or a fresh application of makeup.

Like I said in *Finding a Man Worth Keeping*, we all have a little beauty and a little beast inside. Some just have a bit more beast showing than others. But now you can work on bringing out more of your beauty and minimizing your beast. Does trying to improve yourself mean you have to be obsessed with your appearance and spend hours every morning looking in the mirror? As I said before, that's not how I approached it. But I did make a commitment to myself, and I put in intense effort for a time and maintained the results. Believe me, I was plain Jane. If I can transform, you can transform. I was the same basic person on the inside, just more confident on the outside; and I went from no dates to tons of dates! I have confidence in you, my dear reader, because you do care about yourself and your charisma, or you wouldn't be reading this book. I applaud you once again. Hello, magnetic you!

Automatic Recap

1. No way around it, looks matter in the world we live in. The "pretty people" receive favoritism, including better treatment, and more leniencies. You can resent that or make the best of what you've got to bring out the pretty in you.

2. Magnetic women have charisma, that special charm and appealing personality.

3. Our outward presentation reflects our inward perception of ourselves. What does your presentation reveal?

4. Get in front of the mirror and behold your own reflection. Find and accentuate your beauty assets, while you camouflage, improve, or change your flaws.

5. Follow the three get-pretty-quick tricks: Bathe daily, smile brightly, and stand proudly.

6. This posture secret instantly flattens your stomach, strengthens your core, and shows off your confidence: Make it a habit to suck in your belly button toward your spine, then just lift your head up, and pull back your shoulders.

7. What does the mirror tell you? How is your smile, your skin? Can a little powder do the trick, or do you need a tad bit more time added to your morning routine? Could you use a cosmetologist or dermatologist, an orthodontist or cosmetic dentist, or perhaps even a secret chat with a cosmetic surgeon? You decide.

8. Practice this lipstick trick to prevent embarrassing lipstick teeth: put on your lipstick, then place your first finger in your mouth, close your lips on your finger, then slide your finger back out, removing the excess lip color that may have gotten on the inside of your lips. Then do a quick swipe of

both the top and bottom teeth. Bingo, no more lipstick teeth!

9. You can camouflage any body flaw with the right outfit, so shop until you find what is comfortable and flattering from all angles.

10. Beauty is more than dress size. Eat healthy and maintain a weight that allows you to feel healthy and happy inside and out, and make that your ideal weight. It will be just the right size for the magnetic woman inside and just the right size for your automatic second date!

11. Remember, it only takes a little focused attention on your outward appearance—trim wayward hairs, bleach your teeth, remove moles or warts. It will do absolute wonders for your charisma and confidence.

Are You Ready for Your Close-Up?

Whether your view in the mirror revealed the need for a new hairdo, new outfit, better posture, or even a cosmetic procedure, I hope you were excited to discover that you are beautiful and do possess the charisma needed to complete the formula of a magnetic woman. You are now a charismatic woman, who sees and believes she is a sight to behold. You will now convey that perspective to the men you meet as you continue to take care of the gifts you've been given and diminish the flaws you can't fix. As a fully magnetic woman, you don't deceive yourself; rather, you care about presenting your most attractive self to the world every time you walk out the door.

Automatic Journaling
What Your Eyes Have Beheld

Go to a full-length mirror, dressed as you would dress on a normal day, and give yourself a good looking over for five minutes, and just breathe in whatever comes to mind. Now walk away, pick up your journal, and address these issues.

1. Describe in one word how you see yourself. Is it a negative word? If so, write out the opposite term and explain what you think you'd have to do to believe that opposite term about you.
2. Write out ten things you currently like about your physical appearance.
3. If beauty is hidden from you, what would you guess could use a little attention to bring the pretty out?
4. What is your worst feature? What is your worst figure flaw?
5. When was the last time you changed your makeup, clothing style, or hairstyle? If it's been a while for any of these, today is the day to make a change. Skim some magazines and cut out and paste in your journal a few pictures of people who reflect the image you want to project, including makeup, clothing, and hairstyle.
6. While at work, school, or just walking around today, I want you to observe five people and describe in your journal what you think their posture says about them.
7. Time to play dress up. Go to your closet and pick out three very different outfits that you really feel great in. While wearing each outfit, write down how that outfit makes you feel, and describe the type of person who wears that outfit.

Your Male GPS

How and Where to Meet Men

I n the movie *Monster-in-Law*, Jennifer Lopez's character, Charlie Cantilini, is a dog walker who meets her soon-to-be fiancé in a variety of off-the-wall places before he finally gets up the nerve to ask her out. Their first accidental meeting takes place at a party honoring the dashing Dr. Kevin Fields, played by Michael Vartan. That evening Charlie is a waitress for her friend who's catering the party. The second time, the twosome cross paths at the beach while Charlie is on her job walking about a dozen dogs during the doc's morning jog. The third meeting was at the local coffee shop ordering their morning caffeine. All three encounters are at different everyday locations—same people, different places. Your next first date may be right there in front of you, at your everyday habitual stomps—just open your eyes and look around!

Welcome to the date hunt. Where are those accessible, appealing, available bachelors? I'm talking about the kind of guy who will ask you out and actually pay for a meal. After all, the magnetic woman inside you has just emerged. You now exude a new self-confident attitude toward life. You are primed for a great date. Now where is he? You are definitely ready for a trip to the elusive "meet" market; all you need is a map revealing its location.

I've got that map right here! You see, available and desirable men are already all around you, even if you live in a small town. Somewhere, some place, there are available men within your sphere of acquaintances. You don't have to go out to a bar or nightclub to find them.

You just need to train yourself to consciously pay attention to the human beings who cross your path in the blur of your everyday life. And your newly discovered confidence that has emerged after working through chapters 1 and 2 allows you to open your eyes to the world around you. No longer will you rush everywhere in a distracted state of mind. You now lift up your head, scan the room, and look people right in the eye. So let's get ready to meet your next first date.

There are two primary ways to meet "the boys." One is to come upon their presence on your own, which is the focus of this chapter. The other way to meet potential mates is through setups and blind dates—you know, those special introductions made by other people in your life. Meeting men with a little help from your friends is the focus of the next chapter.

Last Christmas I finally got my very own Global Positioning System (GPS) device! It's not the first time I've used one. Being directionally challenged, I've always made sure my rental cars had one whenever I travel. I just love these things, and now I have one in my car all the time. All I have to do is type in my destination and that nice British voice tells me where to go, door-to-door. When I make a wrong turn, no problem; she just says "recalculating" and steers me from my current location.

Wow, wouldn't it be cool if there were a GPS for meeting men? You know, a date-locator system with turn-by-turn directions that not only told you the location of your next target-rich environment but actually announced where your next first date could be found? Well, that device is right here in your hands. While I can't supply that cool British voice, I can help you develop your own personal locator system—your Male GPS.

Tune In and Turn On Your Male GPS

Have you ever noticed that when you are thinking about something specific, it begins to appear everywhere? Take a new car, for instance. Let's say you are thinking of buying a new car, and you've narrowed it down to a navy blue Mustang. Then over the next week, suddenly everywhere you look you see another blue Mustang driving by. It's not that overnight everyone went out and bought the latest Mustang. It's just that this car happens to be what you want right now, so Mustangs suddenly catch your eye everywhere. Why not make this natural locator phenomenon work for you in finding a handsome, eligible bachelor! Consciously think about the specific type of man you are looking for, and he'll begin to appear seemingly out of nowhere—because you will be mentally in tune to notice him when he walks by! Cool, huh?

Access to your next great date is limited only by your imagination. The two extensive lists that follow—new places to go and new men to meet—does not include every single option. Rather, they are lists to help you get creative as you open your eyes to the many arenas and types of men available for your deliberate yet subtle mission of zeroing in on where to go and who to look for in your search for bachelors eager to bump into a flirting, magnetic woman.

Here's a summary to whet your appetite. You can find bachelors at the town square, trendy diners, your church, the office, the gym, the mall, home-improvement stores, gadget stores, sports arenas, country clubs, art galleries, museums, city parks, charities, universities, concerts, and car shows, to name a few. See what I mean? Men are *everywhere*. You just need to know where to look and then actually *look*.

More good news, just as we saw in *Monster-in-Law*—that quirky romantic comedy—there isn't just one place to meet one particular man. The same well-rounded masculine male can be found at various events and locations throughout his week. You just need to begin to appear at, perhaps, two or three of them—places that are compatible to *your* lifestyle and preferences. Available, exciting men, no matter their professions—be it businessman, clergyman, entertainer, doctor, engineer, salesman, officer, serviceman, singer, actor, politician, entrepreneur, college student, or athlete—all frequent a wide range of locations when they are "off the clock."

Just to give you an idea of the various places you can find the same man, let's look at some of the places, outside his workplace, you might find my businessman husband, using my husband as a case in point. Will frequents college football games, pro-basketball games, concerts, church, sixth-grade church activities (he volunteers), car shows, airplane shows, golf courses, airports (both commercial and private), parks, bike trails, the gym, steak houses, Mexican restaurants, The Home Depot, Best Buy (or any technical electronic store), The Sharper Image (or any gadget store), and more. Whew, I'm already exhausted.

And besides expanding your meet market by going to new *places*, you can also expand it by opening your eyes and tuning in to new *types* of men. There are men in uniform, men in suits, men in swim trunks, men in costume—all kinds of men!

Yes, this takes time and focus, girls. If you want to find more first dates (which of course leads to more second dates), you have to put in the time and effort for your search. You are worth that effort! And besides, we can all use a fun project now and then. And finding your next great date should definitely be fun. Make your Male GPS your current "project," and no one will ever again need to tell you, "Girlfriend, you need to get out more!" because, if you follow the plan in this chapter, you *will* be out more. I can't tell you exactly *when* to be *where*, but I can tell you that the more you are out there, the more likely you are to meet the man of your dreams.

Expand Your Meet Market—New Places to Go

Here's the deal: at the same time you're expanding your meet market by trying out all these new venues and activities, you'll find out what you like and what you don't. When you determine what you don't like, don't go back there to meet men, and you've just fine-tuned your search. Making these kinds of choices will increase your odds of finding a guy who shares your interests and limiting the number of men who don't. But you'll do yourself a disservice if you don't at least *try* new things to widen your horizon. Who knows, you may discover that you're an avid hockey fan or mountain climber, opera lover or Cajun-food connoisseur. You won't know if you don't go.

Now pull out your calendar and block out no less than one hour a week for exclusive male watching, observing the men passing by, as you zero in and connect with the ones who capture your eye. Turn on your Male GPS and get ready for the list . . .

The Town Where You Live

Your automatic second date may very well be right there in the city where you live. Get to know some of these men by learning all about your hometown. A great place to find the pulse of the city is to spend some time at your town center—"Main Street"—which is usually where you'll find the courthouse, library, post office, fire department, theatre, restaurants, banking, and other vital heartbeats of the city. If it affects the residents, most likely it headquarters near Main Street.

Another way to learn about the men in your town is by skimming your newspaper or one of those free entertainment guides found at local restaurants. If you live in a large city, it will most likely have its own monthly magazine like *Los Angeles* magazine, *D* magazine (Dallas), and *New York* magazine. These glossy magazines emphasize the best of the best your city has to offer. Pick up an issue to find out what is "in."

The most convenient and immediate place to research your town is, of course, the Internet. Check out the official Web site for your town (or any city in the country for that matter) by going to a search engine like Google (www.google.com) or Yahoo (www.yahoo.com) and putting in a search for "city of Chicago, IL" or "city of Santa Monica, CA" or whatever city you live in. The official site for that city should come up as an option to click on. There is so much fascinating information to absorb. You can learn facts like current economic level, housing prices, percentage of homeowners versus renters, and much more. Reading up on your community helps you know the concerns and interests of the residents. There's scoop on things to do, places to go, events to see, upcoming housing projects, city news, charity groups, community services, free classes, interesting facts, and so much more. No matter the size of the town, be it one thousand or three million, you can get pertinent information on the city's profile and, thus, the profile of the local men. You can learn who's who, what concerns them, why they live there, when things happen, where to find them, and how much they earn—all with a few clicks of a mouse.

That Trendy Eatery

Another "hot spot" finder is the well-known *Zagat Survey*, in both book and Internet format (www.zagat.com), which offers reviews and price ranges of trendy restaurants in the larger cities.

You can take a girlfriend along or be brave and go solo (perhaps bring a book or work project as a prop if you go alone). If you are broke or a "starving student," add this to your budget as a priority. Scrimp and save your money. Your romantic life is worth it. You don't have to buy a meal. Just purchase an iced tea or an appetizer and water. You are there to see, be seen, flirt, and maybe, just maybe, be in the right place at the right time for that new guy!

The Church

For me, a deliberate and obvious place to search for dates was the church and events sponsored by the church. I wanted a man who shared my passion for a personal relationship with God. Sunday service is not the only time to meet men. Many churches have singles groups, social events, Bible studies, weeknight activities, divorce-recovery workshops, volunteer opportunities, youth groups, camps, and much more. And some denominations have annual singles retreats and conferences, bringing together thousands of singles from across the state or country for a weekend or a week! Talk about a target-rich environment!

We're living in the day of the megachurch. Across the country you find churches with attendance of one thousand, two thousand, even five thousand people a service. A few even have an attendance of more than twenty thousand on an average weekend. With a large church comes a ton of chances for being seen by potential dates, including at singles events, concerts, holiday parties, conferences, Bible studies, choir, and more. Now that can give you a lot of practice in being magnetic! Even if you have to drive an hour to visit once in a while, it is worth trying out an event at one of these megachurches to see who you might meet.

I'm not saying you should ditch your beloved home church and rush out to the biggest church near you just to find a date. But I am saying it is not a bad idea to check out the Web sites of the larger churches in your area to see what they offer singles, and consider trying out one of their events. It couldn't hurt to visit a time or two and see what happens.

Some of us have gone to the exact same church our whole lives (or close to it) and are afraid to venture out to visit another church for fear of betraying our family and friends. I went through those feelings in my late teens and early twenties. I finally had the courage to do it anyway. At first I was so insecure and out of my comfort zone, yet it was great for me to break out and meet new friends. Besides, just because you attend some of the events and programs at another church doesn't mean you can't still go to your own church if you want. Megachurches have a lot of services every week, including at least one on Saturday.

What if the church is of another denomination than you are

used to? Once again, the Internet comes in handy for quick re-search. Not all churches believe the same, that's for sure. Check out the Web site of any church and read its statement of faith or click on its link that says "About Us" or "What we believe." If your differences are minor, try it out. For example, regarding baptism, if you believe in dunking and they believe in sprinkling, that may not be that big of a deal to you. On the other hand, if you believe Jesus is the Son of God and they believe He was just a good man, there is a huge chasm between beliefs that really cannot be reconciled. Know what you believe, get an idea of what they believe, and go from there.

As I confessed in my book *Finding a Man Worth Keeping*, when I first moved up to Los Angeles, I spent time in various singles groups of the local churches I visited before deciding which church to join. Since my church life was of major signifi-cance to me, I wanted to find a place where I could make new female friends as well as find available like-minded men. I don't apologize for that. Certainly, I cared that my place of worship was a Bible-preaching church, rather than merely a positive-thinking university. But if you eliminate the church as a place for romance, you cut out a huge potential of finding men who share your values and beliefs.

The Work Environment

Once a year, the *Hollywood Reporter* comes out with its Top-100 list of the most powerful people in entertainment. Often in that annual edition is found the ten up-and-comers, most likely to be on that power list next year. One particular year, three handsome up-and-comers caught my eye. They also just happened to be producers or executives who would benefit from knowing a few of my clients, so I set up "meet and greet" appointments to pitch my clients. To each meeting I wore a sophisticated business suit and skirt that made me look smart, confident, and feminine. I did my homework, so I came prepared to discuss my clients who were most appropriate for their companies. When I walked into their offices, I made my entrance. I didn't enter in a dramatic and exaggerated "Here I am, come ask me out way"; rather, I walked up to the executive, held out my hand, and gave a warm handshake as I looked him straight in the eye with a warm smile and said, "Nice to finally meet you."

As I sat where I was directed and settled in, I gazed around his office and picked up as many clues as I could about his likes and dislikes, as well as conversation starters. Small talk is so important for establishing rapport. My first comments were, of course, about his recent accolade.

"Congratulations. I must say I was quite impressed. How does it feel to find out you'll be taking over Hollywood soon?"

Eventually I brought up something that I had noticed displayed on the wall, which could have been a sport, important photo, or other accolade. One of the three executives had a few photos of himself playing tennis with various celebrities. To that I said: "I see you are quite the tennis pro. I'm not the best, but I did win best female tennis player on vacation one year. Maybe you can give me some pointers."

After that, my five minutes of flirting was over, and we got down to the business at hand—motivating him to hire my clients. All three meetings with the handsome up-and-comers concluded with offering a handshake one more time as I looked directly and genuinely (*not* seductively) into their eyes, "It was a pleasure to meet you. If you need anything—more information about my clients or anything else that comes to mind—please do not hesitate to call."

Two of the three called me back that very same day. One

called and set up a morning tennis match that turned into a friend-ship and great business relationship. The other asked me for a dinner date that soon became a second date. Flirting works!

What creative way can *you* meet intriguing, available men in your line of work? I mean, nurses have access to doctors. Lawyers, court reporters, and clerks have access to lawyers, judges, and D.A.'s. If you want a certain type of professional, perhaps you can get a job in that field so you can meet men in your line of work!

Dating someone within your line of work gives you instant common ground. You speak each other's language. You'll be an insider in his world. If you want to date someone in the music business, work in the music business. If you want a doctor, work in the medical field. If you want a pilot, work in the airlines, and so on. If you want a writer, work in the publishing or news busi-ness. Clothing designer? Get a job in the fashion world. It's about access.

"Come on, now," you say. "Date at work? Are you serious? I need this job." I'm sure you've heard all the warnings against of-fice romance and dating customers or clients. Can it get messy to mix business with pleasure? Definitely. Been there, done that. Should you think through the consequences before you move forward? Absolutely.

But it's just not practical to completely forbid office dating when you're in your work environment much of your waking hours. Just don't be naive or careless if you need to keep your job more than you want to go out with that guy down the hall.

If you cross the line and mix romance with work, there is no guarantee a permanent romance will develop. Conduct your re-lationship accordingly. Hopefully you'll handle yourself in such a manner that the business relationship can survive, even if the ro-mance doesn't. If an ugly breakup affects others in the office, someone is going to get fired to bring sanity back to the work place, and chances are your guy will stay and you will go. Decide if he is worth it before you dive in.

Having said all that, I've dated clients of my office colleagues as well as several of my customers (executives, producers, and actors). Yet I was able to maintain the business relationships even when the romances faded. The one time it did cause me major grief was when I signed a boyfriend as a client. We were a great team until the relationship ended. I didn't have the luxury of dropping him as a client when he chose to drop me as a girlfriend. He was under contract, and though he wanted the romance to end, he wanted me to stay on as his agent. Uncool and not fun, but I got myself into it, so I had to deal with it.

Sporting Events

Most men love sports. Not all, but most. If you don't mind a sports lover, you will have many men and many sports to choose from. You can focus on the athletes, the fans, the coaches, the organizers, or the promoters. They are all there in the stadium, enthralled in the passion of the current competition. I must forewarn you, however, that when it comes to sporting events, the all-American male is there to enjoy the game, not pick up women. I was a slow learner, but I finally figured that out.

My girlfriends and I went to several different sporting events before we got it that men did not appreciate our attempts at long conversations during the game (with or without including them). Let's see, there were the occasional free tickets I got when my boss couldn't make it to the Dodgers baseball game and he'd give me his box seats near first base. Those were nice seats! And then there was the Clippers basketball game and the Kings hockey games to name a few. Only time we'd get a positive glance would be in line at the concession stands. But when their order was completed, they were off to their seats again.

When we happened to be sitting by cute men, we got the clear nonverbal message that chit chat was to be kept to a minimum and definitely only between plays. Oh, and playing the ditzy blonde who doesn't know the rules is not cute during an important game. Yeah, I tried that too. It's not that it was an act, I really didn't know all the rules, but it was annoying to them to explain when they were focused on seeing every play.

Major sporting events bring out the competitive edge in men. It's great for male watching but not great for gaining a personal captive audience. Go anyway. Sporting events are an awesome playground to study male behavior (both on the field and in the stands) as well as a nonintimidating venue for trying out your new art of flirting. You see, even if you do a terrible job flirting at these events, men are so preoccupied they won't necessarily notice, and it's hard to make a fool of yourself if he doesn't notice you. Practice your nonverbal flirting, and if he notices, great. If he doesn't, chalk it up to something else on his mind, no sweat. Pretty cool, huh?

Now if you truly enjoy the sport and know the rules, then that is an entirely different ball game. You are free to be as vocal and crazy as you want. If it is authentic, being a fan works. Men love it when a lady gets into the game, because it's so rare to find a sport-loving female. Hey, you may even be asked for your number if the team wins and your man is in a good mood. Remember, ditzy blonde, no go; crazy sports fan, yes, big hit.

Here are the benefits of attending major sporting events:

1. Sports offer great opportunities to see and be seen. Where you sit is not overly important. Even if you're in the "nose

bleed section," you can still walk around and be seen at the concession stands.

2. Sporting events are a great place to study male behavior.

3. Attending games expands your repertoire of personal intrigue. It's not a bad idea to read up on the sport you're attending before you go, so you have something intelligent to say if a conversation occurs. Your potential date will be impressed.

4. You get to discover what sports you genuinely like, which ones you can tolerate, and which ones you definitely despise. Once you're married, you already know to plan a "girls' night" on game night during the sports season you despise, and that way you'll remain a happy couple. FYI, making him choose you over his favorite sport is not fair—see, I'm thinking of your future as well.

5. Whether or not you exchange phone numbers at any sporting event, in the very least you are in a venue offering a plethora of flirting opportunities, so you can work on those ever-important skills.

Stretch your cultural taste buds and attend a few ball games. Research these sports on the Internet. Major sporting events include, but aren't limited to, professional football (www.nfl.com), professional basketball (www.nba.com), professional baseball (www.mlb.com), and national hockey (www.nhl.com). Then there's college sports (pick a college and search for its Web site; by the way, all college Web sites end in .edu rather than .com), and minor-league baseball (the Triple-A team owned by a major-league team and usually played in a smaller city—e.g., the Texas Rangers Triple-A team is the Redhawks in Oklahoma City), and arena football (www.arenafootball.com).

The Races

The races are social clubs all their own. NASCAR has a major national following as large, if not more so, than national football and basketball. People travel the country in motor homes and camp out for a week at a time at various races. It's quite the event. To track down the closest NASCAR event, go to www.nascar. com. If you want to check out other forms of racing, it's easily done with an Internet search engine like my favorite, www .google.com. If you are a race enthusiast, want to experience an in-person race, or are simply intrigued by a man inclined to speed, research the upcoming races by using one of the following phrases in your Internet search: auto races, motocross racing, Formula One, Monster Truck, drag racing, etc.

The Country Club

Country clubs are the venue of the quieter sports. Golf and tennis are country-club sports, not exclusively, but primarily. To find what tournaments are in your area, check out these Web sites: PGA golf tournaments at www.pgatour.com and professional tennis matches at www.atptennis.com. If you have discretionary funds in your budget, plop down the membership fee and join a country club near your dream community and learn these sports. You'll be sure to meet a lot of men at the club's golf course, tennis court, or dining room. If you can't afford it, get involved in the nearby charities. Volunteer for their next gala or fund-raiser. It will open doors for you to mix and mingle with celebrities, athletes, high society, and leaders of your community. If you attend any of these tournaments, you'd best learn the etiquette ahead of time. You don't want to be caught chatting loudly at inappropriate times—especially when someone is about to swing or serve.

I had a soft spot in my heart for golfers and tennis pros. I was into the conservative-looking handsome, smart, dedicated guy. One time my girlfriends and I forgot to do our homework when we heard a national golf tournament was coming to town. We were so excited at the thought of seeing dignified and handsome athletes play eighteen holes that we rushed out the first moment we heard of the event and bought our tickets. Much to our chagrin, when we showed up that morning in our best "magnetic woman" golf-tournament attire, we found we had bought tickets for a women's golf tournament. Who knew that the L in LPGA meant "ladies"?

If you are curious about experiencing the sport of the rich and visiting royalty, perhaps you may want to attend a lacrosse (www.uslacrosse.org) or polo (www.us-polo.org) match, which are known as the games of the upper class. You could meet visiting royalty or dignitaries, a CEO of some megaconglomerate, or a bunch of spoiled rich snobs. No matter who you meet, you and your friends can chalk it up as a day to remember.

Special-Interest Groups

Another destination to log into your Male GPS is your favorite special-interest group. Join a group sharing one of your hobbies or passions, such as politics, philanthropy, the chamber of commerce, etc. What do you like to do outside of work? Check out your local chapter for that activity. Your next first date just might be attending as well. Are you into animals, hiking, skiing, or tennis? How about biking, climbing, swimming, dancing, stamp collecting, motorcycling, missions, politics, fund-raising, or charity? There is an organization for everything.

Cultural Events

If you're into the artistic type, you'll likely find him at cultural events, including art museums, memorials, theatre, and the opera. When you go to one of these events, you usually are dressed "to the nines" and look absolutely elegant and sophisticated. They are great places to practice everything you've worked on in elegance, charm, and confidence. I've been to my share of museums and quite enjoy them even when no men are near. It's always good to add a little culture to your life. I've been to two operas. They really do cheer "bravo, bravo" as they softly clap, rather than hoot and holler like audiences at rock concerts.

Trade Shows

Most every industry has trade shows, and since many males are transportation enthusiasts, trade shows for the transportation passion of your individual male is a great place to meet your kind of guy. You might try out the auto show, the airplane show, the boat show, or the motorcycle show. These events happen annually on a local and national scale. To find a show near you, go to one of these Web sites: www.autoshows.com, www.airshows .com, www.boatshows.com, or www.motorcycleshows.com.

Personally, I have always had this thing for pilots (and luckily my husband just happens to have his pilot's license). So here are two extra quick tips: First off, if it's a pilot or aircraft enthusiast you want, the airplane show of the year, every year, happens in Oshkosh, Wisconsin. If you want to meet pilots of every level of training, from military to commercial, jet to prop, charter to private, you must plan a vacation to this show. Trust me, you'll want to book your hotel months ahead of time as many more people attend this event each year than attend each Super Bowl! The

Web site is www.airventure.org. Secondly, many pilots (both commercial and private) started out as military pilots and have many uniformed nonpilot friends in their circles. If you want a man in uniform, it doesn't hurt to have pilots as friends to make introductions.

The Bar Scene

You may have noticed I didn't suggest going to a bar to find available, single guys. I'm not an advocate of picking up someone in that atmosphere. Obviously, it's done every day. I mean, has a quality guy ever stopped at a bar to eat, drink, or wait for his table in the restaurant? Well, sure. But his focus that evening is not on finding the love of his life while he's there. Oh sure, he may be looking for a distraction, someone to get his mind off his problems. But he's most likely not in the frame of mind to meet a quality human being with whom to share his heart. Skip the bar scene, and start out, perhaps, at a local coffee house like Starbucks or The Coffee Bean. Personally, I think resorting to the local bar to pick up men just shows a lack of creativity.

Expand Your Meet Market—New Men to Meet

Maybe you have your heart set on a particular kind of guy, or maybe you're stuck in a rut and only date the same kind of guy over and over and need some variety. Here are a few ideas about how to meet various types of men. After you read through the ideas above and below, even if you don't find your particular hearthrob, you'll have your creativity stirred to the point that you can come up with a plan of your own. Here are some more ideas to keep those creative juices flowing.

Men in Uniform

It was Thanksgiving morning. I was in the middle of my worst migraine headache ever as I drove from West Hollywood to my parents' house in Garden Grove. Able to do little more than focus on the road ahead, five minutes passed before I looked up and noticed the motorcycle cop chasing me with lights flashing. Apparently, I was going a bit more than the forty-five mph speed limit. He was livid.

"Driver's license and proof of insurance!" he growled.

Head throbbing, I looked out the side window at him as I handed over my license. When I caught a look at him, my heart suddenly raced. Wow, he was one of the best-looking creatures I'd ever seen. I tried charming him, but he was too busy scolding me to notice. "Do you realize I have been chasing you with my lights on for the last five miles? How could you not see that? What were you thinking?"

I sheepishly said I was sorry and took my ticket. But I tell you, I could not get that officer out of my mind all Thanksgiving weekend. Despite a three-hundred-dollar ticket, I had a smile on my face that wouldn't go away. On Monday, I not only paid the ticket, I did something impulsive and quite out of character. I wrote a note to the precinct and addressed it to his badge number.

Dear Officer # . . . :

Since I know you feel terrible about writing me a ticket on a holiday, I thought I'd let you make it up to me by taking me to dinner . . . that is, if you're single.

And I didn't tell a soul. I figured if he didn't call, my secret was safe, no embarrassment. However, if he did, my girlfriends would crack up that I did something so utterly crazy. At least we would have something to laugh and talk about for a long time!

He called. We set a lunch date for the following week.

I let my friends in on the secret, and they had great fun tormenting me with the reality that I had no idea what he looked like, not even his hair color! You see, he had on motorcycle attire—large leather jacket, helmet, gloves, and dark sunglasses. Basically, all I saw was his mouth and chiseled chin. What had I gotten myself into? Oh well. I was intrigued enough that nothing was going to stop me from showing up to lunch.

Prepared for the worst, I walked into that Mexican restaurant to meet my officer. And there in the back of the restaurant was one of the most gorgeous men I'd ever seen—now that was a pleasant surprise. Chemistry took over, and what followed was a whirlwind ten-day relationship, right up until the moment he got back with his girlfriend of two years with whom he had just broken up a week before we met.

So I've been out with cops, firefighters, and naval aviators—there's just something about those uniforms (heavy sigh). You just feel so "protected." If you are not anxious for a traffic ticket or rescue from a burning house, how can you meet these protective men? You get creative. Yes, there's the stereotype of cops at donut shops, but that is far from the only place they frequent while on duty. Policemen actually eat at most any good restaurant or café in their jurisdiction (many restaurants are known to have an unspoken policy of complimentary meals to cops. Restaurant managers know it's good for business to have the appearance of security just by the presence of an officer or two in the dining room). If you see a cute officer enjoying a meal while you're at the restaurant, you can practice your flirting skills on him or even come up with some inquisitive remark for an officer of the law—after all, he's on duty, so the least he can do is help out a civilian. And if you want a really fit officer, and you live in a beach community, you can catch a few on their police bicycles. The equestrian type can be found on their horses in places like New York's Central Park.

Here's a unique idea: go to the local shooting range and learn to shoot. You'll meet quite a fascinating mix of men in law enforcement—from policemen to SWAT officers, bodyguards to detectives, FBI to CIA (of course they won't tell you if they are really CIA)—all there to practice their aim. You'll also find businessmen learning to protect themselves. But I must warn you, you can also find a few of those scary types who are a little too obsessed with firearms (and just might be the one you see on the news during an FBI raid of a house filled with weapons and other scary things).

If you dream of a man in uniform to restart your heart, a firefighter or paramedic may be a good choice. Firemen often have intriguing hobbies, extensive leisure lifestyles, and/or second careers since they have unique hours. Their workweek often goes something like this: twenty-four hours on, twenty-four hours off, twenty-four hours on, then forty-eight hours off, or some such combination. And when they are on duty, they sleep at the station. One of the easiest ways to meet a uniformed rescuer would be to work in a grocery store near a fire station. Since they work twenty-four-hour shifts, they shop at the beginning of each shift for the day's three meals, which one of the firefighters will be cooking for the crew. You have a great chance of befriending your local firefighter during a grocery trip. I used to be a grocery checker, and their visits were often the highlight of our week.

One important piece of advice, if you ever happen to meet one of these uniformed men on official business who is absolutely gorgeous, never follow-up with a call to 911 to research the single status of the uniformed heartthrob. A single mom on the

West Coast tried that recently and rather than be humored, the policeman fined her for using emergency services for matchmaking purposes. Obviously, she meant no harm by tying up an important rescue line, but it was a costly lapse of judgment, as well as quite embarrassing when the national press grabbed hold of the story and played the 911 call for the entire country to hear.

Men in Suits

Are you looking for a "suit"? By that, I mean do you want a man who goes to work in a jacket and tie? He could be a lawyer, salesman, manager, account executive, banker, CEO, computer expert, and more. If so, begin to think about where businessmen in your area congregate. Drive around your city's downtown and observe the names on the large office buildings. That will clue you in to the commerce taking place.

My girlfriends and I had the typical schedule of the Los Angeles businessmen down. First, you have to figure their normal workday. For the financial world, hours are pretty consistent— early morning to early evening, with evenings free. Lunch is usually for doing business, either at a nearby restaurant or at a park or comfortable relaxing area with wireless capabilities—such as a Starbucks or business-complex courtyard. You can find public courtyards and dining/shopping centers near office buildings in the business district of any city. Is your office near a business center, or could you schedule a once-a-week lunch in that neighborhood?

If your focus is on a successful businessman, then choose a coffee house in an upscale neighborhood or the skyrise business district. Visit such coffee houses or cafés for breakfast or dinner. The ideal time to visit upscale neighborhood restaurants is on the weekend when many bachelors are "off-the-clock."

Cowboys

Cowboys are the epitome of masculinity and hard to resist. Now, there *is* that song warning mamas not to let their babies grow up to be cowboys. Moms of little girls may have changed the lyrics to "don't let your babies grow up to *love* cowboys." Whether you heed that advice or not, who says you can't at least have some real fun at an exciting event flirting with a man in Wrangler jeans, Justin boots, and that well-worn cowboy hat? Mmm mmm. I don't know if John Wayne and Clint Eastwood cowboy movies had something to do with the appeal of ruggedly handsome men in jeans, but I've dated a cowboy or two, and, believe me, they are charming! Most every one of them has been raised to be courteous and say "ma'am" or "sir." And rodeos are great places to meet these men. If you aren't blessed to live in Texas or Oklahoma or near a ranch somewhere, you may have to find your cowboys at a traveling rodeo. You can find out about the nearest rodeo at www.prorodeo.org.

The Beach Bachelor

There are a lot of beach communities in Southern California where I grew up and spent my dating years. Beaches attract a diverse group of bachelors—from beach bums to entrepreneurs, volleyball Olympians to surfing champs, bodybuilders to break-dancers, Rollerbladers to bicyclists, lifeguards to bicycle cops. My girlfriends and I did our research and figured out which beaches drew the caliber of bachelor we were looking for. (Some beaches had more surfers than Internet mavens, which usually meant less-than-motivated men resided there; so for our personal preferences, we steered away from those waves.) Once we found the beach area for us, we'd Rollerblade, walk along the boardwalk or pier, and frequent the beachside diners.

Celebrities

How do you pick up celebrities—from actors to singers and athletes? When my girlfriends and I wanted to bump into available celebrities, we spent time in their local spots (restaurants, delis, upscale grocery stores, and health clubs) in Malibu, Pacific Palisades, and Beverly Hills, to name a few. Now you may not live near Los Angeles or New York, where many celebrities live, so that may not be an option for you. Yet occasionally studios do offer movie screenings and special premieres across the country. If you find there is a movie premiere near you, those are great opportunities to meet stars. You can try for tickets through your local newspaper, news channel, or radio shows (who might offer contests for free tickets). Also, many of the big movie premieres are sponsored by charities. Try calling the motion-picture studios to find out which charity is sponsoring an upcoming film you want to get tickets to. (You can find out what's coming out by going to www.imdb.com, www.hollywood.com, www.makeitinmedia .com or by going to the specific movie Web site.)

If it's a musician you want to meet, just find out when he will be in town, and see if you can make your way backstage. Ask around. Somebody in your life may know someone who is connected to the man's local promoter, or your local radio station may have access.

Let me clarify that you're not trying to be a groupie or a stalker here! The secret to getting an actual romantic date with a celebrity is *not* to act like one of those; in fact, you don't want to come across as a huge fan at all. You have to act as an equal. You have to be confident. If he thinks you're a groupie or crazed fan, you can forget getting a date.

I was in Nashville for an awards show with several friends. My girlfriend wanted to meet this one singer of her favorite band. A mutual friend thought they'd be a great match and invited us to a pre-award party for his band. Great, we were set. I just knew they'd live happily ever after. My girlfriend was gorgeous, classy, and definitely his type; and he knew he was being introduced to someone that night.

Here's where it fell apart. We got there, and my girlfriend who is frequently around stars and most always composed, got too excited because she was such a huge fan. She just went on and on about his music and how she couldn't believe she was there with him. He did not ask her out.

I'm far from perfect myself. I've blown my share of celebrity encounters, including the time I met Billy Crystal and did my best impression of his famous line, "You look marvelous." To that he rolled his eyes and said, "Gee, I don't think anyone has said *that* to me before." Okay, so sometimes we blow opportunities to carry on normal conversations with people we admire. Just do your best to act normal, realizing they are real people who crave moments of normalcy with normal peers they can relate to; hopefully, that person will be you.

Now, the easiest way to date a celebrity is to work in his world, be an insider, speak his language, and be at the same place at the same time. People like to be around people like themselves, who relate to them and validate them—it's about common bonds. If you want a singer, work in the music world (in radio, for a record label, in production of live concerts, for a promotional group, etc). Want an athlete? Then work in sports, either for a team or media outlet; e.g., if you want to date a Dallas

Cowboy, get a job in the organization. Want to date an actor? Work for a production company, an agency, a studio, an entertainment law firm, a public relations firm, a network, etc. Get the picture?

Men Are Everywhere

Any or all the ideas in this chapter increase your exposure to potential mates and can be explored often. How about deciding right now that once a week you will try one of these options—just one new thing a week—to expand your territory for meeting your next first date—be it attending a singles group, pursuing a hobby, trying a new restaurant, or attending a sporting event. Then once you meet him, take matters into your own hands and *flirt*.

You are looking for available, eligible men—dates who come pretty close to matching the WANTED poster you dreamed up in the last chapter. Study it. Modify it as often as you'd like, and keep that list in the forefront of your mind. Potential dates will begin passing by—and hopefully soon stopping by!

Automatic Recap
Places to Meet Men

1. "Main Street" or your town center
2. Trendy diners and hot-spot restaurants
3. Your local coffee stop
4. Your place of worship
5. Your work place
6. Sporting events

7. The gym
8. Dog walks
9. Home-improvement stores like The Home Depot, Lowe's, and Ace hardware
10. Gadget and computer stores like The Sharper Image, Brookstone, Best Buy, Circuit City, and Radio Shack
11. Sporting goods stores like Academy Sports & Outdoors, Bass Pro Shops, Cabela's, Dick's Sporting Goods, Sport Chalet, and Sports Authority
12. Sports arenas
13. Country clubs
14. City parks and hiking trails
15. Fund-raisers, charity galas
16. Special-interest groups
17. Art galleries
18. Museums
19. Concerts—from rock to pop, country to contemporary Christian
20. Trade shows, like car shows and air shows
21. Universities, colleges, extended-education classes

New Men to Meet

22. Men in uniform
23. Men in suits
24. Cowboys
25. The beach bachelor
26. Celebrities

Open Your Eyes

Eligible men are everywhere; you just have to open your eyes and notice what (or shall I say "who") is around you. It takes effort, self-esteem, and energy, I agree. But hey, you just discovered you are a magnetic woman, so you possess those qualities! Now you are ready to scan the room, search for a bare ring finger, and zero in on his eyes to make contact.

Automatic Journaling
Programming Your GPS

1. Okay, let's see how easy it is to find something once you set your mind to it. Write down your favorite car, including the color and model. The next time you're out and about, I want you to make a mental note of how many of these cars you see. Then tonight, when you pull out your journal, write down how many you saw. What did you learn from this exercise?

2. Write down where you met your last three dates. Was it in one particular place? Did you cross paths with the same guy in more than one place? Write about it.

3. Earlier in this chapter, I gave you lots of ideas about where to set your Male GPS so you can start finding new dates. I'm confident you've already been to some of these places, so today's assignment is to go to a place you already know and try out these new skills. Zero in on your next first date and make eye contact. Record how it went and how it felt.

4. Progressively expand your horizons by testing out your Male GPS further. Starting with the town where you live, go online and check out your city's Web site. Go to www.google.com and search for your city and state. Now read all about your town. Write out ten things you learned about your town, including the male population, the tourist attractions, restaurants, demographics, income level, upcoming events, etc.

5. Next up, let's set your Male GPS to your place of worship, a neighboring megachurch, classroom, or even perhaps, yikes! check out someone in your work environment—if you dare

the inherent risk. Give it a shot, and record how it goes in your journal.

6. Do you live near a lake or park? Visit a popular nature spot near you and check out the scenery. What did you find? Write it down.

7. Visit a sporting event, race, or your nearby country club. How did the male watching differ from other venues? Were there similar men at these places? In what ways were they different? Was it easy to take their interest away from the activity at hand by flirting with them, or were they too interested in what they came to do?

8. What are your interests and hobbies? Write down at least five of them. Now think about what special-interest group focuses on those activities and visit one of their meetings. You can search online for the activity or check out your local newspaper, library, or your town's recreation center. Write down how it went. Did you enjoy the group? Were there any cute guys there? Will you go again?

9. Remember the various types of men we discussed? Choose a bachelor type from that list (men in uniform, men in suits, cowboys, beach bachelors, or celebrities), and make a calculated guess of where that boy may be on his social hour. Then make an attempt to be at the same place at the same time. Record your findings in your journal.

10. Pull out your calendar and choose at least one hour a week to make your Male GPS an automatic part of your life. You don't have to go by yourself; you can bring one or more girlfriends to make it more fun. The more time you put in, the more you'll begin noticing the men around you, and the better you'll get at flirting. Keep a record of where you went and what happened.

A Little Help from My Friends

Welcome to the World of
Blind Dates and Setups

I n the cute movie *Failure to Launch*, Kathy Bates and Terry Bradshaw play parents desperate to have their son, Tripp, Matthew McConaughey's character, finally move out of their home. They find and hire the vivacious Sarah Jessica Parker to attract their son, compel him to fall in love with her, and get him to move out happily ever after. I would say that having your friends or family hire someone to fall in love with you is a bit over the top; however, having them introduce you and set you up on blind dates is a great idea. You just never know—they may be the source of your next first date!

Hey, you've already fine-tuned your Male GPS. And you're stepping outside the box by scanning the room, meeting his eyes, and perfecting those flirting skills. Why not double your navigation field by letting your friends do the hunting.

At times, finding first dates on your own can be exhausting. And it can be intimidating, to say the least. If you are burnt out—or just plain striking out—on finding first dates on your own, never fear; you can always get by with a little help from your friends! In fact, asking my friends to set me up was my favorite, most successful way of getting dates. You meet so many fascinating people this way. And you can ask virtually anyone in your life to set you up. Let's face it. To some degree we are all shy and insecure when revealing our feelings to another. Some just camouflage their insecurity better than others. A little help from a friend goes a long way! So let your friends get involved in matchmaking and take the pressure off of you!

It may not seem that "magnetic" to be set up on blind dates, but you may be surprised at how many people jump at the chance to get involved in your life. This chapter covers everything from blind dates to casual introductions, double dates to triple dates, speed dates to cyber dates, even tips on wedding setups.

All-Access Pass

We all feel a little vulnerable when we step out of our comfort zones and risk revealing our interest in someone. This makes asking our friends for a little help all the more appealing. Having a third party make casual introductions to a potential date is a wonderful nonthreatening way to risk rejection. The man can move toward romance or away from it without being presumptuous or rude. Best of all, if he chooses not to ask you out, you won't experience the typical emotion of rejection, because it was indirect and not in-your-face. It may make you flinch, but you won't fall apart.

Make a list of the people in your life who seem to like you and have your best interest in mind. Who of those folks might have access to interesting bachelors? You can ask your family, friends, coworkers, classmates, church friends, neighbors, pastors, accountant, doctor, dentist, boss, leaders, teachers, etc. I've been set up by my brother, my aunt, a cousin, some clients, customers, classmates, my hairdresser, an ex-boyfriend, my boss and his wife, and a lot of friends. You just never know who has the perfect date for you unless you ask!

Who in your social circle has access to the highly sought after? Who hangs around fascinating people? Who has a unique career or ministry where single men may be found? Who loves to meddle in other people's affairs? You won't know who may be willing to get involved unless you ask! And they don't have to be close friends. One of my friends in Oklahoma met her husband through their mutual dentist who had seen them both within the same week and thought they seemed perfect for each other. The couple married within a year. One year later my girlfriend had her first baby at the age of thirty-seven!

Take a risk and invite people to get involved. It's all in your approach. Make it fun and light. You may not like all or many of the dates, but there's that chance you'll meet the most amazing automatic second date you ever imagined.

I assure you, you'll definitely meet intriguing men you would otherwise miss out on. Personally, I was so determined to find my husband that I had no problem letting the world know I was free. It just made sense to me.

Some girls tell me they feel like losers when they ask friends for help, but it's all in the way it's handled. Sure the guy will know you want a date if a friend sets you up; but the man still has to make the move to ask you out, so the ball is still in his court. And you remain the covert pursuer (remember the magnetic woman's covert motto—chase a man until he catches you!). And you are not asking him out. You are merely letting your interest be known. There is a difference.

At this very moment, there is a flurry of single, available men in this world whom you simply don't have access to . . . yet. Decide to be open to the possibility that there are great dates out there waiting to find you! Now grab your address book and invite some matchmakers to get to work on your life. Here are three, hard-to-argue-with reasons to be set up by friends:

1. You gain an all-access pass to hard-to-meet bachelors.
2. The setup is less direct than pursuing him on your own, so if the guy says no to asking you out, the rejection is not as painful.
3. The guy remains in perceived control and can choose to call or not call; therefore, you have not messed up the balance of pursuer and pursued.

How to Ask for Help

Once you decide to involve others, grab your Wanted Poster from chapter 1. Narrow those qualities down to an easy-to-remember catchphrase of your ideal date. Especially if you're nervous, practice your light-hearted description until it flows easily and automatically. I had mine down to the catchphrase, "Hey I'm looking for the 4 Ss—single, sexy, successful, and saved. Do you know any great guys like that?" When they took the bait, I would explain further if needed.

So just make the decision, and get those in your life involved. Next time you feel the timing is right, give people permission to meddle in your life. You can say something like, "Finding a cute, available man sure is tough these days. Have you seen any lately?" Or, "If you know anyone looking for a gal like me, give him my number." Another approach might be, "Hey, where does a good Christian girl go to find a great guy? I sure could use some help."

You get the idea. I'm suggesting something light and nonchalant as you let the world know you're single and free. If you ask in a fun, nondemanding manner, you will be surprised at how many people jump at the chance to get involved and set you up. Nonetheless, always make it easy for anyone to say no to helping you without repaying their refusal with a guilt trip. No one is obligated to get involved, so if the idea is less than appealing to someone, let it go. This set-up process should be fun for everyone—you, your potential date, and your friend.

Besides, maintaining relationships with the people currently in your life is more important than a one-time shot at romance. If your friends care about you, their decision to stay out of your love life is probably in your best interests. If they don't care about you, then they wouldn't do the best job at setting you up anyway, so don't let it bother you. However, don't stop if someone says no! Ask the next person in your life. Ask a lot of people! I promise, if you keep asking, *someone* will agree to help.

Setups and Blind Dates Come in All Varieties

There are many different types of setups and blind dates—just keep your mind open and your sense of adventure heightened, then get ready for opportunity to knock.

The Casual Introduction

If a full-on setup seems too intimidating at first, try the no-pressure casual introduction in a group setting. A friend invites you and a potential date to the same event, along with several other friends, where you and your perfect match are casually introduced. If sparks happen, romance begins. If there is no pitter-patter, no need to sweat; no one noticed, except perhaps you and the matchmaker. I was introduced to an Academy Award–winning actor this way. My client invited me to join her, the actor, and a handful of crew members after a day of filming at Paramount Studios. She made sure we sat near each other, and we hit it off. It was a blast. Since our introduction was in the midst of a group of people, there were plenty of others to chat with just in case there were no sparks.

Casual introductions are not official setups, so they are non-threatening, yet many sparks have been known to fly. Celebrities who met this way include Demi Moore and husband Ashton Kutcher; and Clint Black and longtime wife Lisa Hartman.

The Blind Date

You will probably be surprised at who sets you up on great dates and who sets you up with complete . . . well . . . mismatches. There's just no rhyme or reason as to why some people are better matchmakers than others. Not all blind dates go well. But hang in there and stick with it. Just hold the attitude that you'll go out and meet someone new and learn *something* about life that evening. Maybe you'll make a new friend, meet your potential mate, or merely end up with a good laugh after the world's worst date. Even if you cry afterward, one day it will be funny. As you can imagine, I've been on every kind of blind date—running the spectrum from horrible to wonderful. I admit that more were disappointing than fulfilling, but I hung in there because there was always that ounce of hope that next time would be *the one!*

One roller-coaster week of dating in Los Angeles will be etched in my mind and my roommate's forever. Date number four with a chiseled-good-looks actor ended early for me when he realized dessert following the meal I cooked him was my homemade cheesecake rather than what he had in mind. Lynn, my actress roommate, was fed up with her own actor boyfriends and was out that evening on the first of two consecutive blind dates with non-entertainment-industry men. This first date was with a Ferrari-driving president of a major corporation, who ended up being a worse creep than some of the actors she'd dated. She came home just in time to see my date storm out and find me in tears in the living room. As we spent the wee hours of the night rehashing our mutual disdain for good-looking jerks, she more than graciously cleaned up the entire apartment, including every pot, pan, and dinner dish, as I just watched. I owed her big time.

Throughout the next day Lynn made every effort to reach her friend who was setting her up on blind date number two— supposedly another successful, good-looking businessman. She was not about to have a repeat of the night before. By the time her date was to arrive, she pleaded with me, "Victorya, we're both blonde. Since you say you owe me big time and you never mind going on blind dates, will you *please* take my place tonight? When this guy shows up, unless for some earth-shattering reason I change my mind, you are going to be Lynn tonight."

I was game. So I quickly put on going-out wear and finished picking up the apartment. As the mystery man drove up, Lynn and I were both taking out the trash. As he pulled up in his BMW M6, the rather striking businessman was greeted by two eager girls announcing "Hi Jonathan, I'm Lynn." Needless to say, we got a laugh that has lasted for years. The "real" Lynn got the date that night, and she and Jonathan have been happily married for more than a decade.

Double Dates

Double dates can be done in many ways. You can choose to have a married or long-established couple join you on your first date, or you can make it a double blind date, where at least two of the folks know each other (such as the girls or the boys). Some people prefer double dates to solo dates because another couple is there to help with awkward pauses. Sometimes, it's more fun to have others involved, because that extra couple changes the whole dynamic. There are two more people to interact with, so the pressure is not all on you to be witty. If one of the others has to go do something—be it park the car, go the restroom, or buy tickets—you are not left alone. If the other couple includes a friend of yours, double dates are also great for getting feedback after the date. If your date turns out to be a dud, having the other couple gives you someone other than your date to talk with. I've been on many double dates, some where I liked the guy and some where I didn't; either way, it was always easy to enjoy the evening because I had someone else to bring life to the party.

Triple Dates

Triple blind dates are a unique, memorable, and really fun way to date. The arrangements and setup can be done by the guys, the girls, or a combination of the two. There are no official "rules," except you do have to figure out who's going to pay. If the girls organize the date, everyone should be told that the evening will be Dutch treat (everyone pays his or her own way); or, depending on the circumstances, you might decide that the girls are paying. For example, if three girls set up the blind dates to an event, it's nice if the girls pick up the tickets ahead of time. It would be kind of awkward for the girls to call three guy friends and say, "Hey, let's all go on a triple blind date. We'll do the setting up, you do the paying." However, equally awkward is preventing the men from paying for anything all night (unless there are no opportunities to pull out the wallet). If the date goes beyond the prepaid event, such as a meal, you can all pay your own tab, or perhaps the guys will be extra classy and decide to pick up the tab.

If your goal is to get an automatic second date with one of these guys, you don't want him to end the evening owing you. You always want to feel slightly indebted to your man. The pursuer is the one who gives and pays. If you want your man to call you back, he needs to feel like the pursuer.

I've been on two very different triple dates, and I have fond memories of both. My first triple date came about when my two girlfriends and I had been wanting to set each other up with various colleagues. Arranging solo dates was just not working out, so one of us finally said, "Hey, let's do it all at the same time as a triple date. Then no one need feel uncomfortable because the guys all know one of us, and we all know each other." It was on.

Christine, Linda, and I each chose a guy to set each other up with. I was set up with a weatherman, I set Christine up with another agent, and Linda got a legal reporter. We were quite the interesting group of six. Since the girls did the planning, we told the guys we were going Dutch treat, and we got together in Santa Monica for some dinner, foosball, and billiards. While there were no love connections, all six had a great time getting to know each other and left making new friends that evening.

Although not technically blind, another triple date I went on was with three guys from my singles group at church. One of the guys was in the military, and they were having an annual ball in Santa Barbara. So along with two of his buddies, they each asked out a girl at church they'd been wanting to date. Mark chose me, Brian chose one of my best friends, and Bret chose Laurie. It was a first date for all three of us. Since it was out of town, the boys rented two hotel rooms, one for the girls and one for the guys. That was one *very* fun date. We were at an elegant, black-tie event. The guys were so funny and charming. It felt like high-school church camp—in a good way. At midnight the boys decided to dare each other to jump off a very cold little bridge into the ocean (ya know, to impress the girls). It was winter, and California ocean water is far from warm any time of year. They couldn't back down in front of each other, so all three did it. It was silly, but they charmed us all. We girls stayed up late in our room chatting about our dates. In the morning the men took us to the Four Seasons Hotel for an elegant brunch. The whole weekend was romantic enough for one of the couples. They ended up getting married.

Wedding Crashers

If you are still not ready to officially ask your friends to set you up, here's a perfect way to get friends involved without blatantly asking—meet a bachelor at their wedding! There is no need to panic at that wedding invitation you found in the mail this afternoon. For too long, single women have dreaded those romantic announcements and have chosen an evening alone with a bucket of ice cream rather than celebrate a close friend's big day. It's time to snap out of that self-absorbed attitude and change your perspective. Weddings aren't just about the bride and groom anymore. They are actually a perfect place to meet your next date!

Don't take a date to the wedding—unless of course you're in an exclusive relationship. You want to be free to be seen as available. Typical guests at a wedding include the closest of friends, family members, and important coworkers. It's a surefire place to reconnect with long-lost relatives and family friends. But it is also a place to meet men who may be strangers to you but are no strangers to the happy couple.

Remember that childhood crush you had on the boy down the street? He's now grown up and just might be at the wedding in your hometown. Live on the edge and make the trip. Or what about that guy you've heard your relatives go on and on about? That wedding you are both invited to is a perfect opportunity to meet him without the pressure of a blind date.

Reasons Weddings Are Great for Setups

1. Weddings are a time for most everyone to dress up, a seldom treat in this era of the casual jeans look.
2. Most guests arrive at a wedding on their best behavior and expect to have a good time.
3. Scoop on that mystery cutie should be easy to get, as somebody there must know him well enough for him to have made the list. Ask around.
4. Conversations are easily jump-started by simply asking, "Are you here for the bride or the groom?"

Get the scoop on the unattached invitees directly from the bride and groom, ideally long before the wedding day. If you ask early enough, the bride and groom will likely be more than willing to spread a little love around by making an introduction or two. You may even get seated next to an available cutie at the reception. If not, as a magnetic woman, you know how to scan the room in a slow sweep, then lock eyes with the one who makes your heart race. It's okay to act as though you are looking for someone specific while you do so, as long as you stop and linger on that one who catches your eye. Don't move on until you've exchanged a smile. Don't rush to your table or even to the restroom. Rather, be deliberate in your walk, casual and slow enough to be intercepted.

So next time an invitation arrives in the mail, don't panic and rush to find some guy to be your escort. Be bold and take a girlfriend instead, or better yet, go by yourself. Your automatic second date just may be waiting near the aisle.

The Contemporary Meet Market

In our busy, demanding world, the art of establishing relationships is getting more and more difficult. But love is a strong force and insists on finding ways to connect. Two of contemporary society's ways of connecting men and women are speed dating and Internet dating.

Speed Dating

If a wedding is not adventurous enough for you, speed dating is certain to push most ladies out of their comfort zones. I would have done speed dating in a heartbeat if it had been around when

I was single. The first speed-dating event took place in late 1998 in Beverly Hills at Pete's Café, the same year I got married, so I was already off the market. You can find some variation of speed dating in many large cities across the country and even internationally. Its appeal is that you have the opportunity to meet a bunch of potential dates in one evening.

Here's how it works: each female participant gets to have a three- to eight-minute minidate with each male participant. The length of the dates depends on the organizer and how many participants sign up. When it is time to move on to your next "date," the host lets everyone know by ringing a bell or clinking a glass. You may not like any of the guys, but then again, you might like them all. The good news and the bad news is that you don't exchange numbers right then and there. At the end of the event, you turn in notes on each of your minidates. The organizers pair up all the couples who mutually chose each other. You could end up with zero, one, or many follow-up dates; yet there is no official rejection while you are there, live and in person.

If you are convinced that you had a major love connection, you just have to be patient until the next day to see if you were correct. Though not a perfect meet market, it's probably worth trying a time or two. It would definitely be a memorable event for you and your single girlfriends to do together. Whether it's a great or horrible experience, it surely can be good for future laughs.

Speed dating is definitely a great place to practice first impressions, body language, flirting, and overall social interaction skills. That alone is worth the ticket price! If you are shy, there are few other opportunities that force you to come out of your shell multiple times in one evening. And if you do horrible on the first minidate, you have several other opportunities to warm up and do better.

The Internet

Okay, okay this is the "in place" to meet people these days. Like speed dating, I got married right as this dating outlet was taking off, so I didn't personally date via the Internet. I don't think I would have had the nerve; but then again, I wrote a letter to a cop who gave me a traffic ticket, so I can't honestly say never.

Sites like www.eHarmony.com and www.match.com are raking in millions and constantly touting more customer weddings. So to say they are popular is an understatement. And it's not just dating Web sites that are big right now. MySpace.com, Facebook .com, Craigslist.org, ShoutLife.com, and other online communities have exploded worldwide and have attracted millions to their sites. Can you meet your husband on the Internet? Yes. You hear of it happening all the time. Here are a few *perks* and *problems* to consider as you evaluate this dating option.

Perks to Online Meet Markets

You gain an instant meet market: by sitting in front of your computer and logging on to a dating Web site, you instantly increase your meet market. You find men in front of your face without ever having to leave your home. You don't have to take a shower, comb your hair, or brush your teeth before going on your manhunt. You just log on to your favorite site and poof! happy hunting.

It's discreet: you don't have to tell the world you need a date. Only your computer screen has to know. So you don't risk embarrassment if you are rejected or no one responds to your profile. Two of my girlfriends who had filled out extensive questionnaires on one of the popular sites were disappointed to get zero matches for the type of man they were looking for within a more-than-reasonable distance. And both of these ladies live in major cities (one in Los Angeles and one in Chicago). Though they were both a little surprised that their ideal man was not currently Internet dating, neither let it destroy her ego.

You get to be picky: the large selection of potential dates allows you to pick and choose. You can cut through the idle chitchat and lay out what you do and do not want in your man. Some sites offer long questionnaires and the ability to request specific criteria to weed out those *not* agreeing with your priorities or possessing your desired qualities.

They are open 24/7: since you can log on anytime day or night, single moms don't need to find a babysitter nor do career women need time off work to shop for the next first date.

It almost sounds too good to be true, doesn't it? That is exactly where I get nervous, because the same online profile could have been written by an honest, healthy, happy hunk or a pathological, perverted, pathetic predator.

Problems with Online Meet Markets

Creeps are out there: just as surely as you can find genuine, quality guys, you will also find some real creeps due to the Internet's impersonal nature and instant accessibility to anyone with a connection and a mouse. These online bad boys run the gamut from simple con men to deceitful married men. You'll also find emotional wrecks wading through messy divorces and, sadly, even alleged "good boys" seeking outlets for a secret dark side.

There's no privacy online: with the ability for anyone, anywhere in the *world* to cut, paste, and e-mail links, there is no such thing as online privacy. If you put it out there, the entire world can read your words or see your photos with the click of a mouse. And with the popularity of YouTube.com and blogging, national media has been known to cover embarrassing stories of private people made infamous by an online presence. That can be horrifying, to say the least. So think it through before you send out any personal commentary, photos, or information.

You cannot easily vouch for the integrity of your cyber pal: you don't know if he is, in fact, married and seeking outside entertainment; you don't know if he is an imposter claiming to be an angelic, devout Christian, when in reality he may very well attend church, but he's got another very unwanted side—he may be a porn addict, looking for someone outside of his social circle, where he can get away with his secret life. He doesn't feel guilty about misleading you because he doesn't think it's personal— you're just an object, a stranger on the Internet with whom he has no real attachment. Beware of this type of Internet man. He is out there more often than not!

You can't read his body language or hear his tone of voice: even highly respected sites cannot verify a person's character. It's hard to catch the bad guys because customers sign up online rather than in front of another human being, and you won't be able to pick up his vibe from nonverbal communication, as well.

Are there bad guys outside the Web? Of course. People are people. I just find that the Internet is the most accessible, thus most frequent, place for these social outcasts to spend their time. Does that mean you should never try Internet dating? No. It just means you need to use more caution than ever when setting up a date in this arena.

Tips for Safe Internet Meetings

Here are a few tips for making your Internet meet market a better experience:

- Don't give out your home phone number, last name, or address.
- Set up a separate e-mail address for seeking dates (e.g., hotmail.com, gmail.com, or yahoo.com).
- Don't give out too many descriptive details. It takes very little information for someone to track you down these days (such as the name of your church, the name of your kids' school, your schedule of exactly when and where you hang out).
- If and when you finally agree to meet, do so at a public place where lots of people are nearby; plus, let a friend in on your plans, and be sure to check in with her when you get back home.

As a very wise writer cautioned in a New Testament letter: "Be self-controlled and alert. Your enemy . . . prowls around like a roaring lion looking for someone to devour."[1] Don't doubt for one minute that the Internet is one of the places Satan prowls. So I caution you, with more than any other form of dating, be wise and alert online. I know I've made a big deal about this, but the bottom line is while you should approach any potential relationship with caution, use extreme caution when exploring any matchmaking options outside your circle of friends, especially through online dating services and online communities such as Craigslist and MySpace.

Extra Tips for the Internet Meet Market

Choose a professional photographer: when setting up your Internet profile, choose a photo that represents the best real you, not a snapshot your buddy took yesterday. A great online tool is the photography service of www.lookbetteronline.com. This company has photographers all over the country who will take your photo at reasonable rates, and they document when your photo was taken so no one will fear it is ten years old.

Covertly pursue your online friend: after you've set up your Internet presence, covertly pursue your online man. Magnetic women let the man do the asking when it comes to the first and second dates. Even if you've begun your dating relationship via online Web sites or e-mails, still let the man lead. Respond when he contacts you, but let him make the move for continued e-mails, phone calls, and in-person meetings. However, don't feel pressure to rush and meet in person until you're sure you are ready.

Consider a background check: consider doing a background check before meeting your cyber pal. For a small fee (usually about twenty dollars), there are companies that will do background checks on potential dates. There are too many companies for me to list here who provide this service. Just go online and Google "online background check" then click on a few of the sites that come up on the search. Typical information that can be traced includes name, address, birth date, marital status, education, employment, income, bankruptcies, liens, judgments, criminal record, and sex-offender status.

Automatic Recap

1. Get your all-access pass to hard-to-meet bachelors by enlisting your friends' help.
2. People love to meddle in others' lives; just give them permission to do so.
3. No one is obligated to help you, so ask in a friendly, fun, nonpushy manner.
4. When your friends take the bait, describe your ideal man with an easy catchphrase.
5. Include your friends by going on double and triple dates.
6. Go to all the weddings you can; it's a great place to meet guys.
7. Be adventurous and try speed dating with a friend or two.
8. If you're curious, go ahead and try Internet dating; just be extra careful.

You'll Get By with a Little Help from Your Friends

A little help from your friends goes a long way! Let your friends get involved in matchmaking, and take the pressure off yourself! It's a matter of perspective. Bosses, doctors, hairdressers, acquaintances, friends, even family members just might have that all-access pass to bachelors you don't know; so open your mind, live on the edge, and enter the world of setups and blind dates. Don't consider setups and blind dates to be less than magnetic. Think of them as hip and adventurous. Dating should be fun; when friends get involved, it adds another fun element. Memories among friends are made, and the pressure is off you to find the man.

Give setups a shot, and try your wish-list catchphrase on some acquaintances. Be ready to be surprised at how many people jump at the chance to get involved, be it for a blind date, double date, triple date, wedding invitation, or even a girlfriend joining you on a trip to a speed-date event. If all else fails, there's always the Internet.

Automatic Journaling
Approaching Blind Dates and Setups

1. Make a list of people in your life who care for you. This can be your family, friends, coworkers, classmates, neighbors, church friends, doctors, leaders, teachers, etc. Just start writing the names of everyone who comes to mind who seems to have your best interest in mind. Then rewrite your list, putting at the top those you think are most likely to say yes to setting you up. You'll be asking for their help first.

2. Revisit your chapter 1 Wanted Poster and narrow those qualities down to a fun catchphrase about your ideal date. Write it down and practice your description. Then take the risk and approach one of your potential matchmakers with your catchphrase and ask about setting you up. Record how it went. Ask another one on the list a day or two later. Keep it up until you have a date.

3. Think of an appealing bachelor a friend knows. Ask that friend to make an introduction for you at an upcoming event. Be ready to flirt and engage in a conversation when the introduction happens.

4. Plan a double date. List some married or established couples you can ask to set you up and be the other couple on the date. Or list a girlfriend or two who would be willing to do a blind double date with you. Now approach one of them to put a double date in motion.

5. Triple dates are not everyday events but certainly fun experiences. Think up a few scenarios of potential triple dates. Ap-

proach your friends about putting one together. Make it a reality.

6. What are the upcoming weddings in your circle of family and friends? What potential bachelors will be there? Ask the bride and groom, family member, or mutual friends about the invited bachelors and if you might be a good match. Keep notes and plan for the big day.

7. Get on the Internet and research the nearest speed-dating event in your area. Call a girlfriend and sign up together. This is definitely something to try just to be able to say you took the risk and did it. Write at least a page in your journal about how it went.

8. Check out a few Internet sites—eHarmony.com, Match.com, MySpace.com, and ShoutLife.com. You don't have to sign up for them. Just explore them and get a feel for how they work. Be sure and follow the precautions listed in this chapter about what NOT to list about yourself if you choose to sign up. Journal how it goes.

Clueless No More

Tips for That First Conversation

I loved the mid-90s teen comedy *Clueless*, where Alicia Silverstone plays Cher, the popular and sweet Beverly Hills high-school girl. Cher's personality seems superficial at first; but as the story progresses, we see that in reality she has charm, wit, and intelligence. As the most popular girl in school, Cher is inspired to take Tai, a "clueless" transfer student played by Brittany Murphy, under her wing to teach her everything she knows about how to get any popular boy on campus to ask her out. In the process, the always-confident Cher actually finds herself a bit tongue-tied when she meets her own love match. Screenwriter Amy Heckerling does a great job reminding us of the insecurity we all face during those first conversations with someone new— no matter how popular or smooth we are.

Do you feel clueless when you get face to face with that guy who makes your heart race? What about when he starts saying things that sound like he may be asking you out, but you're just not sure and you don't want to embarrass yourself. Yikes! How do you clarify? After you've exchanged phone numbers or a friend has set you up, what do you say when he calls? Do you sound excited? Should you pretend you don't know who he is? Have you ever been confused about what to say when someone asks to get together? It can be embarrassing in the least and horrifying at the worst. I know this from experience.

I was nineteen and had a crush on this singer. I had managed to meet him a few times. First time was at one of his concerts, the second was at an autograph session at a local music store, and the third at *his house* at a record-release party. At each of these meetings, we chatted maybe five to ten minutes. Our fourth meeting was backstage at another concert right after he was nominated for a Grammy. I was there with my sister and another girlfriend, and during an autograph session we congratulated him on his nomination. As we were about to leave, he stopped us and said, "I was wondering if I could get your number so we could get together outside the concert scene." It happened so fast and so impulsively that I panicked. I mean, I was very excited, but also insecure and naive. I didn't know if he meant me, my sister, or all three of us, so I gave him all three of our names and numbers on the same piece of paper! How funny is that? He guessed correctly and called my number, discretely asking if I was indeed the blonde—adding he thought all three of us were adorable, but he wanted to have dinner with me.

If these early conversations make your palms sweat, fear not; you are about to be clueless no more. I'm about to teach you how to act and talk during that first conversation—whether it's in person or on the phone.

Are You Asking Me on a Date?

Confused as to whether his invitation is for a casual group or Dutch-treat thing or for an actual date? Come right out and ask for clarification: "Are you asking me on a date?" Yes, you've put him on the spot, but you can recover quickly, depending on his answer; and besides, don't you want to know the answer rather than guess and risk being embarrassed when he shows up or you walk into the party and see you're just one of many girls invited?

If, after his response, you are still confused about whether it's a date or buddy-buddy thing, summon up your flirty side and say, "So, Jason, are you asking me on a date, or do I need to bring my wallet?" You're being light and flirty, so if he meant it to be just friends and says so, you can laugh and say, "I didn't think this was my lucky day." You've now let him know you're open to a date when he's ready, but not devastated. You can still go with him, but expect to pay your own way unless he changes his mind and offers.

As a magnetic woman, you now are learning to pay attention to what's happening around or in front of you. When you're talking to a new guy and he asks you to do something with him, listen carefully to his words. If you are standing in a group of three or more people and he asks you to get together, watch his eyes. As he makes the request, do they include everyone, or is he zeroing in on you? If you don't think you heard him right or if you were distracted at the time, look him right in the eye and say, "I'm sorry I didn't hear you. What did you say?" Don't use a shocked tone of voice, but a light inquisitive tone. If he says, "We're all going, will you go with *me*," he most likely is thinking you'll be his date. If he says, "We're all going, will you *join us*?" it's most likely a friendship thing or he's not ready to take the leap for an official date.

Another way to get clarification is to look him directly in the eye and say, "That sounds fun. Just you and me, or is a bunch of us going?" And remember, your tone of voice matters. Even if he seems like Mr. Confident, he may be putting on an act and barely have summoned up the courage to ask, so be light and easy.

Even if you get embarrassed, fake it while you are in his presence and recover in private. It won't be the last time you turn red. Chalk it up to a learning experience that will bring laughter later.

He's on the Phone, Now What?

The phone call sure has changed in the last ten years. Call forwarding, call-waiting, and cell phones make missing a call almost obsolete. No longer do you have to sit at home pining away for the phone to ring or fear missing a call when you leave the house and go about your daily life. If you want to be available when a call comes in, you can. If you're busy, voice mail can take a message.

Your Greeting

The phone is ringing, and your caller ID reveals his name or number. What do you do? Just answer the phone with your normal greeting, and let him tell you who is on the line. Don't tell him you recognized his voice or saw his number on the caller ID. Let your demeanor reveal you are happy he is on the line, but don't freak out in disbelief that he actually called, even if you are more than thrilled. Simply say, "Hey, it's good to hear from you," or "[Your matchmaker's name] said you'd be calling; nice to hear from you."

Don't be afraid to practice your greeting ahead of time if you need to. Hey, it's okay to be nervous, especially if this will be your first date or first in a long time. Call me a geek, but smooth talking was not automatic for me. I had to work on it. And you know what they say: practice makes perfect. Role-play with a girlfriend or rehearse alone on a recorder. Do you sound at ease, enthusiastic, yet not overly so? That's what you are aiming for.

Let Him Carry the Conversation

After the opening greeting, let him carry the conversation. He may be a "get right down to business" kind of guy, or he may want to chat for a bit to get your vibe. He may also be nervous and struggle with what to say. If a dramatic pause follows for ten to fifteen seconds or so, you may interject with something about how you met or the person who set you up, to jump-start a dialogue, but still allow him to drive the conversation.

Remember, you're waiting for a date request. Don't ramble on and on like we ladies have a tendency to do. Yes, you can engage in the conversation, but keep your answers brief. Respond to his statements and questions with a sentence or two, rather than a bunch of one-word replies. This is not the time to engage in three- to four-paragraph answers though. This is your warm-up for your in-person date. It's an audition, and auditions are best kept brief—leaving him wanting more, not boring him with your entire repertoire.

How Long Should You Talk?

Ideally, keep that phone call somewhat brief. Five minutes is good, thirty is more than plenty. If you think you two have bonded so well that you can't say good-bye, make yourself pause and listen to what he says next. If he's the one keeping you on the line, fine. But odds lean toward it being you who's extending each comment into a full-throttle discussion,

The purpose of this first conversation is to give him a glimpse of how intriguing and witty you are, while leaving him wanting more of you. You definitely don't want to make him hope for a pause, so he can jump off the line. Believe me, it happens. We girls love to talk, while the male approach tends to be more get-to-the-point and move on. So, let him guide the conversation. Respond to his questions with more than a "yes" or "no" but without rambling on every time he says something. You might compare it to a business call, where you start out with idle chit-chat for a short bit then get down to business. Your business on this call is to get down to his request for a date. When you're on the date, you can dive into a deep conversation.

Okay Already, Ask Me Out

Does it feel like he's taking an eternity to pop the question for a date? Is he sticking to safe topics? If the conversation has gone on a bit, and he's just not getting to the point, you can help him out with a leading statement. If you haven't yet met in person, you could say something like, "It's nice to get to talk to you; I look forward to meeting you." Then pause and wait for his response. If you've already met in person but you haven't had a date yet, then say something like, "It's great to hear from you; I look forward to getting together." Then let him respond. If he mumbles something like, "I hope to get together soon," say, "Sure, when?" or "Sure, what works for you?" But leave it at that if he doesn't pop the question from there.

If at any moment he says, "Well, I won't keep you," or "I've got to go . . . ," pause and let him finish what he was saying—it may be his moment to get to the point. You don't want to interrupt and talk him out of asking for the date.

It's okay if your first phone call ends without a scheduled date. Annoying maybe, but not fatal to the relationship. You want him to do the asking, so let it go and say good-bye. You've let him know that if he drums up his nerve again and calls back, the door is open. Most likely he will take the lead and schedule something right then.

It's Been One of Those Days

Not every first conversation is going to go perfectly. You might have had a bad day at work or have a very unattractive stuffy nose or just say something that comes out wrong. It happens. That doesn't have to mean you blew it.

If you've had a bad day, don't advertise your drama to your new guy. He doesn't need the whole story; and trust me, he doesn't want it. Your date doesn't have the luxury of knowing how wonderful you are yet. Telling him all your problems may scare him off. That doesn't mean you have to be fake, just don't whine on and on about how everyone is out to get you.

If you're in a funk, don't take the call. Let him leave you a message. You're probably not in the frame of mind to make witty comments anyway. Best to return the call when you feel more "on" for charm and romance. If you *do* take the call and he asks how your day was, be honest, but don't go into graphic detail of your trauma. Say, "It's been one of those days; work is crazy right now." Or "Everything that could go wrong did go wrong today; but hey, it's better now that you called." Or "The kids chose today to try my nerves, but I lived to tell about it," or some very light summary of your dilemma followed by a laugh. This call is not meant to be a free therapy session, so don't put the pressure on him to fix your problem of the day.

Is the Conversation Going Downhill?

I could so relate to Will Smith's character in the movie *Hitch*. He went to extremes to transform from a geek to a chick magnet. He was so successful that he became a relationship expert (sounds like the male version of me). Yet his smooth act was fragile. When he let his guard down and allowed a particular woman to sweep him off his feet, that old insecurity crept back under the surface, tripping up his words and confusing his thoughts. Not because he was a geek, but because he was human and got nervous. Yes, I know he was just a movie character, but he showed how so many of us feel and react. We're not perfect, and sometimes things go downhill.

Let's say that a phone conversation is not going so well—awkward pauses become unbearable, or his answers seem silly or off the wall. You begin to think, "Oh no, I may have a geek on my hands." If by midway through that conversation you are wavering about whether you should say yes or no to a date, err on the side of yes. Chalk it up to nerves on his end, and give him the benefit of the doubt. No matter how "cool" your guy seems with his friends, he may still get insecure and nervous with girls. Take it as a compliment if he is insecure with you in your phone conversation. Then see if he comes to life when he sees you in person.

If your first phone conversation is awkward because he is insulting, vulgar, or antagonistic toward your values, that is another story. Don't bother accepting a date. In that case, it's best to stop any potential romance before your heart blocks your brain.

However, if he's not a proven creep, don't believe someone is not good enough for you until you've given him a chance. The public seemed shocked that David Spade, an actor who often plays a geek, could possibly be dating gorgeous actress Heather Locklear. *That must be some kind of joke,* many thought. Truth is, those who know David Spade know that off screen Spade is a funny, cool guy with a lot of savoir faire and charisma and a long list of beautiful and famous ex-girlfriends. Don't fall for first impressions. Give the guy a chance, and see what happens once you get to know him.

If the conversation gets off to a less than great start, you might want to have the first date be a lunch or early evening date so you're not locked in to a full day or late night.

He Popped the Question!

Once he asks for the date, respond with a light, "Sure, what did you have in mind?" or some other appropriate reply, and go from there. If you want to keep the date on a restricted time line, a lunch date is a great way to go. At most, you spend an hour to an hour and a half together, and you don't have to stress as much about running out of conversation topics. A dinner date usually lasts longer. You can expect an evening date to last about three hours. If you get together on a Saturday or after church on Sunday, the potential time together is even longer. This is good or bad depending on how well you two connect and how comfortable you are spending that much time on a first get-together. Keep these time frames in mind when making plans.

If you already have a conflict in schedules, don't automatically cancel your other plans. If he wants to date you, he can wait until you're free. Having things going on in your life is not necessarily a turnoff. Men like women who are hard to get. If you're not available, then say so; but make sure he knows you aren't blowing him off. You could tell him, "I'd love to, but I've already got something planned. How about a rain check?" (By the way, you're not obligated to tell him what your other plans are.) Your specific response will depend on what he asks you to do. If he asks you to accompany him to a concert or special event, going another time may not be an option, so you can say, "I'm so bummed I'm going to miss it. I'd love to see you another night, though; even though I'll obviously miss the show." Or "This week is crazy, but next week is good . . ." then let him take the bait.

What If It's for Tomorrow Night?

If your guy calls on a Thursday or Friday for a weekend date, it's best to say you've got plans but would love to see him another time. You want to get the message across, without saying it plainly, that you are popular and need to be booked early in the week if he wants to see you in the coveted weekend slot.

Again, you don't owe him an explanation. Your plans can be as boring as watching TV, doing laundry, catching up on work or homework, writing in your journal, or cleaning your house. Just be sweet and say, "Oh, I wish I could—it sounds great—but I already have plans. Can we make it another time?" He has to want to see you bad enough to plan ahead.

You are not scolding him or telling him it's not respectful to call you at the last minute. No sir. You're getting your message across covertly by implying you are busy and hard to get. If he wants to capture you, he has to book you early.

It's very important you *don't* say something snippy like, "I can't see you tonight, you didn't call me early enough, and a lady doesn't accept last-minute dates." That will shout out "game player." Let him figure it out on his own—not because you're game-playing but because you are establishing that you are worthy of being thought of first!

Your man will not respect and value you if you are available at any moment's notice. If you drop everything for him, you send the message that he is everything to you and nothing else in your life matters. That should not be the case, especially on the first few dates when he does not merit the status of someone so important to you. Definitely don't cancel on friends. That is rude to your friends and, again, sends the message that preplanning with you is not necessary. Magnetic women are smart, active, and have friends they value. Just because a date enters the picture does not mean you change the way you treat your friends!

Where Shall We Meet?

Shall you have him pick you up at your home or meet you at the place of the date? It really depends on your comfort level, how you met, and how well you know him. How did you meet? Were you strangers with no common friends? Then it is a very good idea to meet at a designated location, so you have your own car and he is yet to know where you live. It's not the rule, but a good idea. If you have checked him out and have a high level of evidence that he is not a stalker, thief, or psycho, you can let him pick you up at your home (if you are not a single mom, because moms need to be extra protective of their children). The benefits to having your own transportation are that you can leave when you want, he doesn't have to know where you live, and you don't have to worry about whether he's a good driver.

I once endured an hour's drive home from a concert with such a bad driver that I prayed fervently the entire way. About an hour after we parted, he called to let me know he had totaled his car as he smashed into a stalled car on an off-ramp. He had just missed killing the two former passengers of the stalled car as they had managed to leap into the bushes as his screeches began. Not everyone is that dangerous, but be aware that your life is in someone else's hands when you get into his car.

How and When to Say Good-bye

After he's asked you out and made arrangements, it's time to end the conversation—no matter how much you still have to say. Save it for your date. Again, you want him to look forward to spending time learning more about you, not feeling as if he's getting together with an old friend about whom he knows everything. Keep the first phone conversation brief. After he's locked up the date, say, "I better get back to . . ." or "I've gotta run, but it was sure nice talking to you. I'm looking forward to seeing you." Politely excuse yourself from the conversation, and start thinking about your upcoming date.

Automatic Recap

1. When an in-person invite is offered in a group setting, watch his eyes. Is he looking at the group or directly at you. Does he invite you to "go with us" (friends) or "go with me" (date)?

2. If you aren't sure he's asking you to go as a date or as a friend, just ask with your most flirtatious delivery. If he says "as friends," just lightly laugh and say, "Okay, I'll bring my wallet."

3. If an upcoming phone call is making you nervous, practice your greeting to ease your nerves and build your confidence. Role-play with a friend to see if you sound at ease.
4. Let him carry the conversation. Don't give wordy dissertations to his questions, but don't give only "yes" and "no" answers either, or he'll think you're a bore.
5. Keep your first phone call brief—five to thirty minutes is plenty. You want him to get to the point and ask you out, so don't get sidetracked with a long conversation.
6. When he asks you out, offer a pleased and affirmative, "Sure, what did you have in mind?" or "I'd like that, when?" or other appropriate reply.
7. If you're not available, don't automatically cancel your plans. Tell your man, "I'd love to, but I've already got plans that night. How about a rain check?"
8. Don't feel bad if he doesn't ask you out on that first call. Some guys like to test the water before they jump in. Still leave it in his court to do the asking.
9. If you're in a bad mood, don't answer the phone. Let it go to your voice mail.
10. Give your man a chance even if the conversation seems like a dud. He may just be nervous or intimidated. Think of it as flattering.
11. Don't accept last-minute dates. If he asks you out for a weekend date on a Thursday or Friday, it's in your best interest to say you've got plans, even if you're just doing the laundry.
12. Based on how well you know your date and your own comfort level, decide whether you want to meet him someplace or have him pick you up at your place.
13. After he sets up the date, politely wind down the conversation by saying something like "I have to go now. I look forward to seeing you" or "I better get back to . . . It was nice

talking to you." You want him to leave wanting more, not less, of you, so keep that first call short but sweet.

No Longer Clueless

Whew, that wasn't hard, was it? Now you know exactly what to do and say on that first phone call. If this part of the dating process used to make your palms sweat, you should now be confident and dry because you are ready to pick up that phone and accept your next first date.

Automatic Journaling
Stopping Cluelessness

1. Pull out your journal and write out one of your "clueless" moments when you met a potential date and you crashed and burned. Write in as many details as you can, from what you said to how he responded. When you are finished, imagine how it could have gone, ending with your getting the date. Now rewrite your experience with that positive outcome. What would you say and do if you could live that moment over again?

2. Write out three potential clarifying responses for when that bachelor asks you out. Record yourself practicing, or try it out with a girlfriend to get her feedback. Make sure you remain light and flirty. Tone of voice matters. You don't want to come across as demanding or snotty.

3. Write out a few greetings for when your man dials your number. Keep it friendly and light and remember when answering your phone, you want to let the person identify himself rather than advertise you saw his name on caller ID. Feel free to record yourself practicing your greeting, or you can practice with a friend until you are comfortable.

4. Since we ladies usually love to talk, take a few days to monitor your conversations. On the first day practice holding back a little. Throughout your day really notice your conversation with anyone and everyone. Do you tend to be long-winded and answer every question with a five-minute monologue? Or do you respond with one-word answers? Pay attention and write notes.

5. On day two of observing your conversations, answer ques-

tions in the normal course of your day with one- to two-sentence answers, then wait to see if you are asked for more details. If the person asks for more, go for it; however, make sure you pause often enough to allow the other person to participate. On the other extreme, if you have been giving only one- or two-word answers, spend the day trying to expand your answers more descriptively into one or two sentences. Record how it goes. Did it feel awkward? Did people appear more interested in talking with you? Keep working on your chatting skills.

6. On day three, time your phone calls. Notice if you are guilty of keeping people on the line longer than they seem comfortable with (and of course you don't want to do that with a new date). In addition to timing your conversation, consciously add pauses every five minutes or less, and wait for the person to "make the next move" to see if it is you who is dragging out the phone call. If he or she keeps it going, fine. But I warn you, people may be trying to wind down and you keep jumping at their every word to expand their latest comment into another hour.

7. Write out three responses you can give your potential date if he asks you out at the last minute (e.g., "I'd love to, but I already have plans," etc.). Say the lines aloud. Do you sound convincing? Are you charming rather than condemning?

On Your Mark, Get Set . . .

Getting Ready for That First Date

I n the cute romantic comedy *Maid in Manhattan*, Jennifer Lopez's character, Marisa Ventura, is a single mother from the Bronx working as a maid in New York's fancy Manhattan hotel district. By a twist of fate, a handsome senatorial candidate, Christopher Marshall, played by Ralph Fiennes, falls in love with the beautiful but "lower class" Marisa. The politician is swept away by the hotel maid's elegance and beauty when he walks by a room she is cleaning right after she has tried on a gorgeous gown left behind by a wealthy hotel guest. When Marshall sees Marisa in the beautiful dress, he mistakenly thinks she is a socialite. Marisa effortlessly pulled off her right-dress-at-the-right-time encounter. In the real world we're usually not that lucky; in fact, we often spend hours deciding what to wear.

First dates are notorious for shaking up a bundle of nerves—combining fear of the unknown, hope for a happy-ever-after, fashion anxiety, and memories of dates-gone-bad. Anticipation keeps you clinging to hope that *this time* he may be the one. Add a blind-date element to the mix, and you push the adrenaline up another notch, because there is just no guarantee your blind date will remotely resemble the hype from "reliable" sources. Believe me, I have been shocked at some of the contrasts between the descriptions friends gave and the reality of who appeared. But then again, I have been more than pleasantly surprised with other dates who were given only mild descriptions. You just never know until you go. The combination of nerve-wracking elements is what makes first dates larger than life. It's what keeps you in the game.

With all that pressure from the start, cut yourself some slack and increase your chances for a great date by following the practical tips in this chapter to help keep the date going smoothly: (1) dress appropriately for wherever you go, (2) know some basic dating etiquette, (3) be prepared with back-up plans, and (4) expect to have a great time no matter what happens.

Dress for Success

Let's be honest. Most every woman agonizes over what on earth to wear on a first date. But there's good reason for our concern: clothing defines us, even when it's a mistaken identity. Our clothes are a large part of our personalities and image. Your mission is to look and feel fabulous the minute you finish getting dressed. It's not so much what you wear as it is how you wear it. So dress first to please yourself, then to please your date—because if you love how you look, you can't help but shine, and your date will notice. You can find something fabulous for any dress code, be it casual, athletic, business, or formal. You're not going for overkill; you just want him to see you and smile.

The Message behind the Hemline

No pressure here, but other than your wedding day, a first date is one of the most important events for choosing the right outfit. A lasting impression of you will be etched on his mind the minute you open the door, before you've even said a word. Your man will size up your personality, begin figuring whether you fit into his life, and decide, if you do, what form of relationship it may turn into. Will you be a friend, a fling, or forever? Your style plays a large role in that decision. Set the stage by dressing for the message you want to proclaim, realizing your clothes also represent your values.

Too many girls mistakenly buy into the fashion-magazine fairy tales and believe that the only way to get a guy to call back is for him to want you passionately and immediately—hence, they go the revealing, sexy route. Oh, you'll capture his attention this way—as well as everyone else's in the restaurant—but you'll engage his mindless lust, not tug his heart. When you ponder what to wear, keep in the forefront of your mind that we are going for a *second* date, ladies, not a one-night stand. Of course, you want him to be attracted to you, but you want him to see you as a person, not an object. The Pamela Anderson look is not what you're going for!

One of the good things about the social foibles of celebrities like Britney Spears, Lindsay Lohan, Jessica Simpson, Carmen Electra, and Paris Hilton is that they regularly show us what *not* to do, how *not* to act, and even what *not* to wear—especially if we want dates to think of us as more than conquests. Of course, these fashion-loving trend setters do get it right sometimes. We end up buying copycats of the glamorous gowns they wear to premieres, award shows, and red-carpet galas. We also buy less expensive replicas of the street clothes that cameras catch them in while they visit Starbucks, Malibu cafés, or go on Melrose shopping trips. It's these gals' *nightlife* attire and antics that lack judgment.

Mariah Carey is another celebrity whose hemline choice reveals her insecurity. The record-breaking singer has more than earned her popularity as a brilliant singer and songwriter. Yet the moment a young crop of pop stars arrived on the scene, she changed her style to compete with their sexy images. I was embarrassed for her recently when she was seen in South Africa for the opening of Oprah Winfrey's Leadership Academy for Girls, the school for needy girls. While most celebrities who flew over showed up in conservative attire, Mariah stood before the cameras in a cleavage-advertising garment that seemed to scream "Look at me, look at me!" Gals, if you think all you have to offer are your physical assets, you are not a magnetic woman; you are insecure.

Risqué party-girl fashions draw gawking stares from the male species; and yes, your date may be all over you with lust, but he will not stick around, treating you with dignity, even if you are a world-famous celebrity. These starlets may look like they're having fun in pictures splashed across the tabloids, but they keep getting dumped by Hollywood's bad boys. No matter who you are, one of the laws of the universe is that you've got to respect yourself to command respect.

Do You Know Where You Are Going?

Your fashion selection will be much easier if you know where you're going before your man shows up. Since what you wear depends on where you go, find out what your date has in mind and what *he* plans to wear. Do his plans suggest casual, trendy, or formal threads? You're not trying to be his clone; you just don't want to be in jeans if he's in a tux.

If he reveals the name of the restaurant, you can always call the restaurant yourself to get an idea of the dress code. Some of the upscale restaurants don't allow jeans, so check it out. Are you headed for dinner and a movie? If so, comfy and nice casual is a way to go. How about wearing your favorite jeans or slacks with a trendy top or classic blouse? Then maybe add a blazer or leather jacket, and you're set. In the summer you can show off your tan and toned legs with a stylish sundress and sandals.

If you're not sure, ask, ask, ask. Yes, there will be some first dates who will remain elusive about their plans, which can be frustrating. If you can't get the details, ask for the dress code.

As soon as you have an idea of the anticipated dress code, choose not only what is stylish but what is comfortable on your body so you won't be distractedly fidgeting all night. Don't forget about the weather either. Spaghetti straps may look great, but you won't be having fun if you're freezing. And who wants to worry about pulling your skirt down every few minutes or constantly adjusting your blouse so you don't "fall out"? No matter how fabulous an outfit is, if it's uncomfortably tight, itchy, or awkward, you will be so preoccupied shifting in your seat that you won't be focusing on all those skills you've been working on thus far.

In Defense of Flats

If your guy is planning on taking you to an amusement park, outdoor concert, sporting event, or long stroll at the beach, three-inch heels won't be your friend. However, if it's an opera or classy restaurant or any place where you won't be walking much, you may prefer those leg-flattering heels. Remember, you want to focus on your date, not your sore feet. Yes, heels make your legs look longer and prettier, but you may have bad knees or feet that would make long walks less than romantic.

On the same theme of comfort, I have to admit that I find some gals' attire humorous at college football games. These ladies certainly have the outfit selection down pat, many showing team spirit along with trendy sportswear. What makes me laugh is that some of the young gals choose toe-pinching high heels rather than hip tennis shoes. I admit they look great, but it's not fun to walk for miles across the parking lot to the football stadium then up the long ramps to your seats. My feet hurt enough doing that in comfy tennis shoes; and besides, your shoe choice is not going to make or break your chances for a callback if your man picks a football game for your date! I bet his shoes feel good on his feet!

The Cozy-Wow Factor

Though comfort is paramount for a relaxed evening, there is little excuse for wearing frumpy, unflattering clothing just because they're in style or cozy. You can find outfits with style and comfort that also flatter your figure (at all angles) no matter your size. Just keep shopping. Keep trying on clothes until you find that cozy-wow factor. And don't let the price tag freak you out. These days discount options are endless, from outlet malls to department-store specials, from Ross and T.J. Maxx to Burlington Coat Factory and Marshalls, from boutique clearance sales to consignment shops.

Here's a little secret for the fashion challenged: if you're buying a new outfit, go to the mall and select something off the mannequins. (I've definitely done it!) The clothing stores put their latest and greatest on those stands to draw you in, making it easy for you to see what's hot. You can also ask the sales gals, as most folks working at those boutiques love fashion and are eager to share their expertise with you.

Bottom line, when your man shows up, you want him looking you over and thinking, "This gal is for me." So here's one more secret (which we'll cover more thoroughly in chapter 8): it's called "mirror, mirror." Automatic second dates are gained by making your date feel liked and at ease with both you and himself. When he's with someone just like him, he feels accepted and, thus, comfortable. Clothes can do this! Just mirror the style of clothing you think your guy will wear. Dress like him! If he's into cowboy boots, wear cowboy boots. If he's going to wear shorts, wear shorts. Dressing in similar fashions subconsciously tells him you like him, you *are* like him, and it's natural for you to be together. In other words, you validate your man.

You don't have to be a fashion expert. Just dress in a manner that reflects your date, flatters your assets, and diminishes your flaws—all while allowing you to forget about your clothes once you've put them on. Tall order, I know, but not an impossible one. Make a decision, get dressed, then spend all your energy on your date rather the status of your buttons, zippers, and hemline.

Mind Your Ps and Qs

Cell-Phone Etiquette

Cell phones are both a blessing and a curse. No matter what you think of them, they are clearly not going away. And observing cell-phone etiquette is an important requirement for a first date.

Make sure you turn your cell phone to mute. If you are expecting an important call or you are a single mom, place it on vibrate, and let your date know ahead of time that you may get a call from your babysitter. Don't be rude and answer a call unless it is really important (we all have caller ID these days). Every time you take a phone call when in the presence of another, you've made the definitive statement that the person in front of you is less important than the person on the phone. It certainly doesn't feel great when you're the one left sitting silent while your date spends time on his phone. The New Testament offers simple wisdom for this—and other behaviors in dating for that matter—"Do to others as you would have them do to you." [1]

Pardon the Interruption

If you're a single mom, make arrangements so that your kids will not interrupt your date unless it is a medical emergency or for some other agreed-upon reason. It's not always easy for kids to handle their mom's dating, so don't be surprised if they do all they can to interrupt your date. If you've taken care of their basic needs for the time you're with your date, they do not need to interrupt you or even call you at bedtime to say good night. Besides, as a mom of two young kids, I know how ineffective a bedtime call from mom can be: being on the phone and being in person are two different things to your children. I'm not saying you can't call if your child truly only goes to sleep when Mommy says good night. Just forewarn your date you'll be making that call. Also, for the sake of your children, don't introduce your new man on a first or even a second date. The kids should be protected from getting attached to your new love until you've established a secure relationship. It should not affect their lives until he is a potential permanent fixture.

The Moment of Truth: Who Pays?

When the bill arrives, that little slip of paper can be like the elephant in the room. Ignore it anyway. You are his guest; he will pay (unless you asked him out, and then it's not really a date, anyway). By paying for your meal or tickets, your man feels good about himself as a provider and protector. It makes him feel needed. Don't take that away from him, especially on the ever-so-crucial first and second dates.

Even if you obviously make more money than your date, let him pay for the evening anyway. He can choose an evening that fits his budget! It takes a confident woman to allow a man to be her leader and provider, but I know you have it in you. Dr. John Gray puts it this way: "When a man receives the message that she doesn't trust him to fulfill her needs, he feels immediately rejected and is turned off."[2] Unless he's a freeloader, he won't be calling back for a second date. Refusing to allow a man to pay for you is not simply being polite or considerate; rather, it's revealing a mistrust of your man's ability to provide for you tonight or ever. Not a good message.

If you are the one who asked your guy out for the evening, then there is a good possibility that he is approaching this as a friendly get-together rather than a romantic encounter. Plus, if you did the asking, you are either each paying your own way, or you, as the inviter, are paying for the evening. For the first and second dates, I still believe it is best that the man do the asking. Down the line, when you're in a relationship, or after at least three or four dates, you can invite him to a concert or sporting event if tickets just happen to land in your lap. But don't ask him out for romantic encounters early on if you want him to pursue you!

If I haven't been crystal clear on this yet, let me spell it out plainly and clearly here. On a first and second date, all bills should be covered by the man. He pays. You receive. He pursues you. You are pursued. So how do you prevent the awkward feelings when the bill arrives? Should you *offer* to help out or perhaps pay the tip? No. That is why he chose the restaurant and the activities for the evening. He chose; he pays. If he asked you where you want to go, it would be a good idea to have a general idea of how much he wants to spend. If you have no idea, say, "What did you have in mind, something fancy, trendy, or casual?" "Fancy" generally means expensive, "trendy" restaurants are usually in the medium range, and "casual" diners are the least expensive of the three categories.

If your date does not immediately jump on that bill, leaving you so uncomfortable you fear you'll faint, then it's time for a trip to powder your nose. Excuse yourself for the restroom; check your makeup, relax, and be gone for a solid five minutes. That is plenty of time for your date to notice the tab and settle up. My girlfriends and I used this trick often, and it always worked!

On the weekend triple date I told you about in chapter 4, the other girls started freaking about how the guys were paying for everything and felt pressure to pay for breakfast. But hey, breakfast was a four-star brunch in Santa Barbara. I bet that tab was higher than the gala the night before. Needless to say, I wasn't feeling the same pressure. My friends' discomfort began showing on their faces as the boys let the check linger, so I stood up and invited the girls to the restroom. Those girls spent those five minutes squirming, laughing, and debating me on my antics; but I held firm. And, of course, we went back to find the boys had, indeed, paid the bill. One of the girls even commented, "Oh, you guys paid for breakfast too?" and one of the guys said, "We were waiting for you to pick it up, but then you ran to the restroom." I just smiled and said, "You guys sure know how to treat the ladies.

Thank you for such an elegant breakfast." They were charmed and that was that.

I know we women have been encouraged to exert our independence, and this advice sounds old-fashioned compared to our current social male-female interaction guidelines. But I'm telling you, allowing men (those you want to date, anyway) to be in the role of provider makes them feel good about themselves, and it works.

Green Eggs and Ham

Let's say your man has arrived and smiled approvingly as you opened the door. You've won his heart, thus far, with your style. But now he tells you you're headed for someplace you don't think you want to go.

However, before you insist you don't like something, make sure you're not pulling a *Green Eggs and Ham* moment—you know, shooting it down before you've even tried it. We've all been guilty of this at some point—pouting and spouting something that resembles the famous line from the Dr. Seuss favorite: "I do not like green eggs and ham, I do not like them Sam-I-am." My husband still gives me grief for refusing to try Maggiano's spinach salad with him on one of our dates. I finally broke down and took a bite, and yes, just like Dr. Seuss's Sam-I-am, I figured out it was delicious. So now whenever I say no to anything, he just looks and me and says, "spinach salad!"

If you haven't tried the opera, hockey, or rodeo, be adventurous and go anyway. It's good to expand your horizons. If it's an ethnic restaurant you've never tried, even though it sounds disgusting, go anyway. One of the few legitimate excuses for shooting down a restaurant is if you're allergic to most of the items on the menu or if you got sick there on your last visit. And I will say it's not rude to refuse calamari, oysters, or monkey brains if the thought of putting them near your mouth makes you gag.

If you think sports are boring on TV (and you've never been to a game), you need to live a little and go to experience it live. One date took me to my first hockey game. Though I hadn't enjoyed it much on TV before, I went anyway and had quite a fun time. I even got to see the legendary Wayne Gretzky play in his last season.

First dates are about trying new things! If you end up hating it—fine, don't do it again. And certainly don't pretend you love it if you hate it, or you'll be deceiving both yourself and your date! That's unfair. A friend's first wife pretended to love everything he loved (from sports to music to outdoor activities) all the way through the honeymoon and then abruptly let him know how she really felt as soon as they unpacked. Needless to say, the marriage didn't last, both ending up feeling hurt and deceived!

Plan Ahead

You've asked the questions, you know where you're going, and you've decided what to wear. But you're still uneasy. First dates can be nerve wracking for a number of reasons. One of the best ways to make yourself more comfortable is to do a little planning before the big date. I'm not saying you need to try to orchestrate the whole evening, but having a plan can relieve some of your worries and free you up to have fun.

Friends Suddenly Appear

You can always enlist a little help from your friends on first dates if you think you need it. I don't recommend it for all encounters, but it's an idea for blind dates or dates you are dying for your girlfriends to meet so they can give you feedback. Here's what I did: on occasion, certainly not always, I would arrange for some friends to just happen to be at the same place at the same time to bump into me and my date and say hi. I've had blind dates do this to me as well. It's great to meet his friends and have your friends meet him in a casual, subtle, "accidental" way; then you both get feedback.

But how do you handle this with a goal of getting a second date? If you're going to have your friends appear, have a plan laid out for them to just as slyly disappear. Prearrange a cue for when it's time for your friends to leave, even if your date politely says, "Sit down and join us." Trust that they'll follow your lead. If you let your friends know they need to leave, they need to follow the plan and leave so you can get back to one-on-one. You shouldn't have to figure out how to tell your friends to get lost.

No-Plan Stan

What if your guy shows up at your door and doesn't have anything planned, then asks you what you want to do. Yikes, what do you say? It may be time for Plan B. While it's always ideal that this conversation has occurred before he shows up, that doesn't always happen. So I recommend keeping a Plan B in mind, being aware of his budget so you don't suggest places out of his price range.

When asked where I wanted to go on a first date, I always suggested a trendy and relaxed restaurant, because you're placed at a table where you can relax, order comfort food, and get to know the person in front of you. And believe me, you learn a lot about a person's character in the restaurant environment. How does he handle the wait staff and the entire dining experience?

Do you have to have back-up plans? No, but it's a good idea. Being prepared can make an unbearable evening tolerable or, better yet, transform it into a fabulous evening. Do your research on your hometown and surrounding cities and find out what the community has to offer. A Saturday hike near the famous Hollywood sign was a hit with a visiting businessman, and sparks flew as we gazed at the large homes around us and shared our dreams for the future. That businessman became my husband!

Movie Night

One of my dates chose Steven Spielberg's award-winning film *Schindler's List* for our date. Sure, I had wanted to see that important picture, but it wasn't exactly a romance-inducing movie. That powerful, must-see film left me and my date utterly speechless when we walked out of that theatre door. The evening couldn't recover from the heaviness of the message, so he just took me home. Our pairing survived more dates, but a lesson was learned by both—no deep, heart-wrenching films early in romance.

Movies are not the ideal for a first date, yet there will be times a date makes the theatre part of his plans. What do you do when your man suggests a popular movie you have no desire to see? No problem, just be prepared with what you'll say when he springs the news on you.

If you know it's going to be a movie night, check out what's currently playing at your local theatre. What are the plots, the themes, the reviews, and the ratings? All this is easily accessible at many Web sites (including moviefone.com, movies.com, and pluggedinonline.com, to name a few). Your local newspapers and weekly magazines have reviews too. Once you know what's playing, come up with at least two alternate movie suggestions, just in case your date doesn't like your first backup choice. When your man announces a film on your "won't watch" list, don't immediately assume his morals are in the toilet. Maybe he's just listening to popular hype or merely has different taste in movies (many men prefer action over romantic comedies). Keep your request for a change of plans light and friendly, not sour and negative. Lightheartedly tell him you prefer something else by saying something like, "Oh, I'm not really into that film, how about . . . ?"

You're going for a good time, no matter what, remember? So try not to judge or make him feel bad for suggesting a less-than-desirable flick. Just practice what you'll say and offer other choices. If it's a movie you heard only mediocre reviews on, maybe you should give it a try anyway. But if it's a film opposing your values, you don't have to go. Same thing if violence disturbs you—you just don't have to go to those action flicks. Be prepared in case your date suggests a heavy, crude, horror, or violent movie out of your comfort zone, so you can be ready to speak up with that Plan B.

If you can't come up with a film suitable for both of you, suggest another idea altogether. You can say, "Why don't we skip the movie and do something where we can chat at the same time." You might suggest miniature golfing, paint-it-yourself pottery, the arcade, bike riding, hiking, the amusement park, sightseeing, the zoo, or a local tourist trap. The ideas are endless—just be prepared and be creative.

Now you can look forward to your next movie date. Just read movie reviews and know what you'll say before the date. Being informed and having other options will not only save you embarrassment, it may just get you that second date.

Murphy's Law

After a long absence, an old flame reentered my life and invited me as his date to the MTV awards, held that year at UCLA's Pauley Pavilion (a basketball stadium) in Westwood, California. I put in the time and found just the right outfit along with the perfect purse and heels. The evening arrived, and we settled into our seats. When Nirvana and lead singer, Kurt Cobain, finished singing "Lithium," host Dana Carvey announced that Guns N' Roses with frontman, Axl Rose, would join Elton John for a duet of one of Sir Elton's hits right after the commercial break. I chose that break to sneak off to the restroom in the dark. Big mistake.

Ever notice how bad memories are recalled in slow motion? One missed step on those unlit arena risers, and I fell, sliding down past more than a dozen aisles, knees first, totally scraping up my shins. I remember praying, "Please, someone, help stop me." Like a playing card clipped to a bicycle wheel, hands kept reaching out, slapping me as they attempted to slow my tumbling descent down each step. When I finally came to a stop, droves of people, including my date, rushed to see if I was okay.

Okay? Of course I'm okay! Just don't talk to me right now. I'm so humiliated, I'd rather die.

"Yes, thanks, I'm fine. I'll be right back," I said, holding it together without shedding a tear. I quickly excused myself and went to the restroom to evaluate the damage to my stinging legs. What appeared were shredded nylons and two very unattractive scraped and bloody legs, from my knees to the bottom of my shins. I would have wallowed in my pain a bit, but inside the same restroom were two other girls in the same blood-streaked predicament. It was so pathetic; all three of us just met eyes and laughed. That was the first and only year MTV held the show at that venue.

The moral of one of my most embarrassing moments is to be prepared for the unexpected! Did I have a back-up pair of nylons in my purse or Neosporin for my wounds? No! What about pain relievers and Band-Aids? No! How I wish I had. That was the last time I didn't.

You can learn from my mistake, as well, and come prepared for whatever little mishap comes your way. Yes, I had a funny story to share at MTV's after-party; I certainly stood out. But aside from being painful, it was rather unattractive and embarrassing to be all dressed up from the knees up and look like Halloween in April from the knees down.

When packing your purse, make sure you include little things that may come in handy. If you spill something on your clothes, it helps if you have a pouch of Shout Wipes to keep the stain from settling in. If you end up with a flat tire, an auto-club card comes in handy. Bring extra hair accessories as well, in case you want to change your hairdo at some point. Don't forget a credit card for emergencies, at least twenty dollars cash in case you're caught at a cash-only place, and two dollars in quarters in case your date doesn't have change for parking. Benadryl is great for unexpected allergic reactions. Be creative, and fill that purse with some saving grace. You'll thank yourself in the morning. I promise.

May I Take Your Order, Please?

While working on this chapter, I happened to go to Pei Wei, one of my favorite Asian eateries. Writing in restaurants is one of my quirks. While enjoying my Asian chopped-chicken salad, I began getting animated and inspired as I ferociously typed along on my keyboard. I'm sure the three iced teas had something to do with my jittery clumsiness, but whatever the reason, I dropped a chopstick three times. Each time I glanced around the room, hoping no one in the crowded lunchroom had bothered to notice; and each time I caught the same amused gentleman in the corner of my eye. Oh well, what could I do? I looked over, shrugged my shoulders, and smiled. As he and his wife were leaving, they came over to laugh with me as he shared a similar experience he went through in China. When all else fails, smile in the face of your embarrassment. Your date will be charmed that you are less than perfect.

Dining disasters happen, but here are a few tips to help you either prevent them from happening at all or at least turn any that do into a minor mishap. Visualize what you want before you order. How gracefully will you be able to eat that entrée? Will you use a fork, chopsticks, or your fingers? Will it be messy to eat? Try to choose items that are small or able to be cut small and picked up easily with a fork. Some foods are just messier than others. Large-leaf salads, triple-decker sandwiches, and four-inch-thick hamburgers are hard to eat gracefully. BBQ ribs? Forget about it! Lobster and crabs? Well, they're so tasty they may be worth the work involved to get each bite out of the shell.

Do you suffer food allergies? Definitely don't keep that a secret. Let your date know and have your own dosage of epinephrine in your purse just in case your allergic item is an unknown ingredient in your meal. Benadryl works on many allergic reactions (check with your doctor first). Next time a date brings you to a restaurant, think through that menu with the thought of graceful eatability as well as flavor, and you'll save yourself from one more red-faced moment.

Keep on Moving

Even if you both have the most amazing charisma, something can still go wrong on a date—especially a first date. It's how you handle those little bumps in the road that determine the success of the evening. Your first date doesn't have to go smoothly for you to get another. When things go wrong, just go with it and do your best to laugh at yourself. You will laugh later, so why not now? And if the glitch in your plans is something horrible like a car wreck, just be calm and understanding, because your date won't be thrilled his car is smashed. Adopt my brother Dave's mellow approach and say, "It's all good." Go with the flow and make the best of it.

After all, there's a bright side to every date. For one, you're spending time with someone new. That alone is worth celebrating. And maybe . . . just maybe . . . he will not only turn into a second date, he may turn into a mate.

Automatic Recap

1. Clothing defines you; choose your outfit according to your desired message.
2. Remember, it's not what you wear, but how you wear it. Make sure it's comfortable.
3. Ask about the dress code and try to dress similarly to your date.
4. Don't go broke shopping for the perfect outfit; shop sales, outlet malls, and discount shops.
5. Remember, the man pays, you receive.
6. Be prepared with a Plan B for various budgets.

7. If you run into friends, make sure they know when to leave.
8. Research the movies currently at the theatres.
9. Pack your purse for emergencies (cash, credit, Band-Aids, aspirin, Benadryl, etc.).
10. Choose the least messy menu items for graceful eating.
11. Go with the flow.
12. If you expect to have a great time, you can turn lemons into lemonade!

Smooth Sailing

With all that pressure inherent with first dates, cut yourself some slack and increase your chances for smooth sailing by following these logical and easy tips. Dress for success, mind your p's and q's, be prepared, and look on the bright side of whatever happens—and you'll be on the road to your automatic second date.

Automatic Journaling
Going from Get Set to Go

1. Project time: Go through your closet and separate your clothes by dress code—from casual to trendy, church, formal, and so forth. Once you do that, pick one dress code at a time and try on each outfit. Discard the uncomfortable and unflattering clothes (or at least segregate them to a section of your closet of nothing-else-to-wear-I'll-just-settle-for-today clothes. If only a few outfits remain, it's either time to shop or time to trim down. Write down how this made you feel.

2. Once you've reflected on the clothes in your closet, pick out five outfits and write a sentence about the personality and message of each particular outfit. Is that the message you want to radiate? If so, keep it; if not, time for the giveaway pile.

3. Today, notice ten gals who walk by you throughout the day, and write a sentence or two about the personality and message each outfit projects. If any are messages you want to put out there, go to the store and pick out a similar style.

4. This is a fun game to do with family or friends: pick out various outfits at a clothing store, and have others guess who it reminds you of. This is a great way to realize we really do identify people by their fashion sense. Write about this experience.

5. Going back to your closet, pick out the most favorite outfit you own. Try it on complete with shoes and purse. Now walk around your home, sit down and stand up, cross your legs and lean back on the couch. How do you feel in this outfit?

Are you able to relax, or are you having to fidget to keep everything in place? If the latter is true, I recommend you save this fabulous outfit for date three or four and not date one or two. Your man will be pleasantly surprised to see you dazzling as the relationship progresses, and you won't be as stressed, so a little discomfort for fashion's sake is okay at that point.

6. Mannequin-shopping day: grab a girlfriend, or just have a shopping day for yourself, and try on only the outfits you find on the mannequins and in the window displays of the stores. Take one of those outfits home. Write about the experience.

7. Time for a little couple watching. Observe five romantic couples today. Do they dress in similar styles or colors? Write what you find.

8. Time to live a little. Think about some things you think you dislike, be it food, spectator sports, movies, or sporting activity. Write down why you don't like it. If your reasons are not etched in stone, decide to give it another try, especially if a date suggests it.

9. List the friends you'd like your next first date to meet. Chat with each of them and plan how to have them miraculously appear at the same place as you and your soon-to-be date. Write down the plan so it can be revisited before the big date.

10. Make a list of Plan B suggestions for the three price ranges—casual, trendy, and fancy. Get creative and have a list of five to ten in each category.

You Had Me at Hello

Conversation Tips for the First Date

Remember that unforgettable scene in *Jerry Maguire* when Tom Cruise comes bursting back home to Renée Zellweger in the middle of one of those at-home girl meetings? All the other ladies at the gathering just sit there in awe, staring as Cruise's character Jerry Maguire goes on and on, ending with those precious words "You complete me." At that moment, Zellweger's character, Dorothy Boyd, stops him to say, "Shut up. You had me at hello." Ah, yes, he was there, face to face, doing the one thing she wanted most—being there in her presence. Real life doesn't always turn out like the movies. Yes, being there in person is rather crucial for a relationship to begin. But it's in those very moments that your words play a vital role in moving a relationship forward or stopping it in its tracks. And sometimes we all can use a little conversation savvy to help us move beyond "hello."

You've captured his attention and finally made it to the first official date. Hurray! Your doorbell is about to ring, or you are about to hop out of your car and meet him at that restaurant. It's time to inspire your new man to think, *You had me at hello!* and compel him onto the road of ultimately believing "You complete me." If all goes well, your date is going to be convinced that spending this time with you is the best decision he's made all year. As hard to believe as it may seem, it is actually and honestly possible that you, yes you, can make that happen on your first date. All you have to do, after you've got that boy to show up, is make this first date all about *him* rather than you!

There are two deliberate reasons to take the focus off you and make this date all about your man. The first is that this method ensures your guy will have a great time because you'll be focusing on his favorite topic—himself. Talking about him is a powerful yet covert way to compel any man to leave your presence thinking you were the most fascinating lady he's met in a long time. And he won't know it has a lot to do with the fact that you merely discussed things *he likes*, rather than rambling about your interests or trying to prove your worth.

The second smart reason for making it all about him is that the sooner you learn about him, the sooner you'll find out if he is worthy of you, something too many women fail to discover until way down the line where many hearts lie in ruin. Oh, but not you. You will not be one of the heartbroken statistics. No no. You're going to be different, because you will find out about this man right up front in the midst of showing him a great time. Both this chapter and the next ("Let the Sparks Fly!") go into detail about all the little things you can do to master the art of making the first date all about your man.

Off to a Good Start

Start off on the right foot from the moment you say hello. "All about him" includes valuing the time he's carved out for you. Be different from the stereotypical female and shock your date by being ready when he arrives. Being late is a rude habit. Separate yourself from the pack and make a great first impression by showing that you value his time simply by being ready when he gets there. If by chance you are late, salvage your faux pas by groveling. Offer your excuse with a sincere apology rather than acting as if nothing happened (which is also rude).

The Art of Conversation

As your best magnetic self, you are covertly using your expertise in the fine art of communication, which means that tonight you will be a reporter, psychologist, politician, and admiring fan, all wrapped up in one. We're ready to delve into the art of conversation and learn everything to say on a first date without offending your man—from superficial warm-up talk to prying, personal questions. Wow, that's a tall order, but you can do it. I have faith in you! Just look into his eyes, begin with safe small talk, then guide the conversation toward your date and his interests. Actually listen to the answers before you respond. You want to gain his trust, extract information, hear all his stories, share only your intriguing ones, and divert him away from topics you're not ready to discuss.

Gaze into His Eyes

Throughout your conversation, show genuine interest in your date by looking him in the eyes whenever he is speaking to you. Don't glare obsessively or stare freakishly. Rather, offer a gaze of focused attention and genuine interest. Your nonverbal message is, "I am listening to you, even though we are in a room full of people. You fascinate me."

The Formula

Here's the secret formula—ancient words that still work today: "Everyone should be quick to listen, slow to speak and slow to become angry." [1] The relevance, especially on a first date, is to be quick to listen to all his stories, slow to bore him with wordy details of your stories, and definitely slow to reveal unresolved, bitter anger over your current or past relationships. Sounds simple, right? Well if you put your mind to it, actually it is. Just focus on your date and ask him questions about his life, then actually hear his answers and respond on topic.

Look, it's not rocket science to know that men love to talk about themselves; don't we all. You are just going to help him do so. Just don't be insincere in your interest; your body language will give you away if you try to fake it. And your man will know you're a phony and lose your number. Besides, there's really no excuse for being uninterested in his stories on a first and second date because you need to know about this guy to (1) find out what fascinates and bores him and (2) see if he's the right guy for you. So get your mind off yourself and focus on your date. You're not just doing it for him, you're doing it for you!

If he gets on a topic you are far from an expert on, don't open your mouth and insert your foot. Tell him you don't know much about it and ask him more or change the subject. Draw out his interests and get him talking about things he likes, be it sports, music, business, or his dog. You can learn more by listening and occasionally interjecting another question than by doing all the jabbering, on any day.

The Reporter and the Psychologist

The skills for charming a date are no different from those used to establish rapport in the work place or social circles, even with celebrities and world leaders. Legendary reporter Barbara Walters agrees that you begin any new relationship by showing personal interest in who the person is. If the focus is *not* on your new friend or guest, you will not be establishing instant rapport, period, be it with dates, interview guests, or anyone for that matter. "Do not talk excessively about yourself at all in the beginning," says Walters. "Even if you're an older woman and unmarried, it does not require an explanation. Take it easy on the personal confessions. It will come out as time goes by, when the relationship is well enough established, that the skeletons in the closet will be considered amusing decor."[2]

Like a good reporter, ease any anxiousness about spending time with someone new by doing a little research and preparation. Successful interviewers do their homework on their subjects before their guest arrives. Whether it's a reporter doing his own research or a TV anchor relying on the segment producers to do it, that interviewer has prepared the questions before the show. Ease your anxiety by doing the same before your date. Come up with some questions you want to ask before you go.

Don't worry if he announces he feels like this is an interrogation. Just laugh and say, "Oh my, does it really? I'm sorry I'm asking so many questions. I just find you fascinating and want to know all about you." Let him ask the next question, relax, and lighten up on your approach. You'll get better at this in time.

Here is where the reporter meets the psychologist. You see, you are not setting out to merely interrogate your man to see if he matches your "list"; you are seeking to really hear what he says in order to get to know the person inside. A good psychologist is master of this skill of seeking to understand by asking questions and really listening to the answers. A great listener does all four of these things: look, listen, repeat, respond. In other words, *look* at him when he talks, *listen* to what he says, then *repeat* what he says in a brief summary to see if you understand what he's saying. Wait for his acknowledgement, then *respond* with one of three things: (1) a nod encouraging him to continue, (2) another question for him on or off topic, or (3) a story about your life on the same topic.

An important part of this interview angle of dating is to realize that everyone wants to be heard. Blend the skills of a reporter and a psychologist, and really listen to your date's answers, then show you are listening by following up with questions or comments related to his answer. Then definitely bring up similarities from your life to show you share common ground. Don't be busy focusing on the next question immediately after you spew out your current question. A conversation builds one response at a time. If he just told you about growing up on a farm, you can mention where you grew up or tell if you've ever been on a farm, but following up with a comment about your favorite perfume or his favorite car does not exactly sound like you've been listening to what he's just said.

Here are one hundred questions to get the reporter in you going:

1. Did you see that story about . . . ? (current headline)
2. Can you believe this weather?
3. What was the weather like where you grew up?
4. What do you prefer: hot, cold, or moderate?
5. What relaxes you most—the beach, the mountains, the plains, or the arctic?
6. What is the farthest place you've ever traveled to?
7. Where is your favorite vacation spot?
8. Where were you when . . . ? (life-stopping national headline of the past)
9. What was the last natural disaster you lived through?
10. What do you think is worse—earthquakes, hurricanes, or tornados?
11. Where are ten places you'd like to see before you die?
12. What do you like to do in your free time?
13. What are your all-time favorite three movies?
14. Did you ever walk out on a movie? Which one and why?
15. What are you three all-time favorite TV shows?
16. What were your favorite TV shows growing up?
17. What are your current favorite TV shows?
18. Who's your favorite musical group?
19. What CD would your friends be surprised you own?
20. What blast from the past would your friends be surprised you own?
21. Have you ever been to the opera?
22. What's your favorite food?
23. What your favorite hobby?
24. Would you rather Rollerblade, surf, or snowboard?
25. Who's your favorite sports team?
26. What is your favorite sport?
27. Do you play that sport on a team or for fun?
28. What sports were you into growing up?

29. Ever make the newspaper as an athlete?
30. What's your favorite college team?
31. What's your favorite professional team?
32. What is one of your talents?
33. What would people be surprised to learn about you?
34. When did you get your first cell phone?
35. How old were you when you got your first car?
36. Was it old or new?
37. Did you buy that first car, or was it a gift?
38. Are you a night owl or early bird?
39. Are you a schedule person or a go-with-the-flow person?
40. Are you a hunt-and-peck guy or a serious keyboarder?
41. Day-Timer or PDA/iPAQ?
42. Do you enjoy your tunes on an iPod or CD player?
43. If and when did you get your first traffic ticket? Your last one?
44. Tell me about your scars.
45. What was your first broken bone?
46. Have you ever had to stay in the hospital?
47. What was the best thing that has ever happened to you?
48. Have you ever been on TV, in print, or on the radio?
49. Do you keep a journal?
50. Do you write music, poetry, or stories?
51. Do you cook?
52. Are you artistic?
53. Tell me something about you that your friends don't know.
54. Tell me about your family.
55. How many siblings do you have?
56. Are you close to them?
57. Are your grandparents still alive?
58. What was your relationship like with your dad?
59. What was your relationship like with your mom?

60. Which relative are you most like and which most unlike?
61. What is your favorite memory growing up?
62. What was your favorite Christmas surprise?
63. What have you kept from your school years?
64. Were you a geek or prom king?
65. What was your first pet?
66. What was your favorite pet?
67. What did you want to be when you grew up? Did that change?
68. What was your first job?
69. Ever work at a restaurant?
70. How did you get where you are today?
71. What led to your current job?
72. If you didn't have your current job, what would you do?
73. Describe your dream job.
74. Who had the most influence on the person you are today?
75. Do you make future plans or just wait to see what comes your way?
76. Where do you see yourself in five years?
77. Where do you see yourself in twenty years?
78. What are your top five goals for your life?
79. Do you plan on having kids?
80. What is the funniest thing that ever happened to you?
81. What is your most embarrassing moment?
82. What has been your proudest moment in life so far?
83. What makes you happy?
84. What makes you sad?
85. What breaks your heart?
86. Who turns you off?
87. What turns you off most?
88. What scares you?
89. What makes you angry?

90. Who impresses you?
91. Who are your heroes?
92. Do you consider yourself political?
93. Growing up, what was your view of God?
94. What is your current view of God?
95. Is faith important to you?
96. What is the meaning of life?
97. What is one thing you wish you could do over or take back?
98. If you could change a stranger's life, how would you do it?
99. If you could change one thing in this world, what would it be?
100. If you were given one million dollars to spend within twenty-four hours, how would you spend it?

Being "In the Know"

Another way to slowly but surely build rapport and show off some easy-to-come-by intelligence is to begin your date with safe "in the know" chitchat. A great way to educate yourself in what is happening in your mutual world is to be familiar with current news. You may only know a headline, but the fact that you are up on something timely will make an impact on your guy whether he tells you or not! Want to look like you know more than you really do? Get the headlines before you leave for your date.

You don't have to read every story, just know what is generally going on in the news when you show up for that first date. There are three ways to do this: catch the nightly news; read the daily newspaper; or my favorite, get free daily headlines e-mailed directly to you by major news sources, including major newspapers, local newspapers, television networks, and special-interest organizations. Just by signing up with your e-mail address, most will e-mail you alerts when breaking news happens. So you don't even have to be watching TV or listening to the radio before you go. Just go online and check your in-box. Here are some of the free Web sites to check out: www.usatoday.com, www.latimes .com, www.nytimes.com, www.people.com, www.msnbc.com, www .cnn.com, www.christianitytoday.com, and www.focusonthefamily .com, to name a few.

Being "in the know" makes you appear more intelligent and interesting. And if you don't check out the headlines on a regular basis, at least do it the day of your date. Scan the headlines and read up on a few stories so you have something current to talk about beyond the inevitable comment about the weather.

Another way to increase your perceived intelligence and prevent yourself from returning a blank stare when current events come up is to make sure you know basic politics and who the current leaders are in your world. Who is your president, vice president, governor, and even your mayor? What is the current political crisis in this world, and who are the major players? Smart people know what is going on around them and how it affects them. You don't have to have deep knowledge or advertise any of it, but having it fresh on your mind helps you carry on a conversation relevant to the day.

It's a bonus if you know his line of work ahead of time so you can do a little research and get the headline in his work world. You don't have to spend hours doing so; hopefully he'll share all the gory details if he finds his work worthy of discussing, but if you can interject some knowledge, that is a plus.

Me Too!

But what about you? Can't you share anything about your life? No need to feel left out when you follow my formula of making the first few dates about your man. I am not saying you cannot share anything about yourself or tell any of those fun and exciting stories about your life that you'd love to reveal. You are simply letting him be the *focus*, while you guide the conversation where you want it to go!

How do you bring up one of your exciting moments? Start with questions on the topic of your favorite stories. Listen to his experiences on the topic, then counter with yours when the timing occurs naturally. If you have a specific story you want to share about something that happened on a vacation, ask him questions about vacations he has been on. If you want to share a story about how you got the job you have today, ask him about his career path. If you are dying to tell him about your appearance on a game show or an honor you received in the newspaper, ask him a leading question on a similar topic.

Keep to the short version of your stories, expanding to the longer, more-lively version only if he asks for details. It may be wise to practice your stories by either writing them down and practicing aloud or telling them to your friends and getting their feedback prior to your date. That way you can see if your delivery is as exciting to the listener as it is to you, the storyteller. Telling stories and jokes are a natural talent for some. We all have friends who can make a trip to the library sound like an invigorating trip around the world. Others, like me, have to work on our delivery of timing, punch lines, and dramatic pulse. It's not the experience that is boring; it is the retelling of the event that often fails to intrigue. So work on your delivery.

As you engage him in telling his stories, it will become obvious to you which of your related experiences bring out the common threads in your two lives. You are looking for the "aha!" or "me too" moments that will draw you together like two peas in a pod.

You Fascinate Me

When you share your life stories, you're going for the memorable *wow* factor—not to intimidate, but to intrigue. What is unique about your life? What are some silly family traditions worth mentioning? If these things don't come up naturally during the evening, turn them into questions when a pause occurs, such as, "What was your favorite meal your mom cooked?" or "What is one thing your family ate growing up that people laugh at when you serve them now?"

My family always had popcorn whenever we ordered pizza, and we added sliced dill pickles to our homemade tacos. I didn't realize that was odd until I tried serving it to others when I grew up. People are often taken aback, yet some actually enjoy it. Who knows, I may have started new traditions across the country. So what about you? What new things can you introduce to your date's life?

Okay, okay, I heard what you just said. You are not dull! You have done more exciting and unique things than you realize. You just need to dust off your memories. Stop and think. What are some things you want to reveal about your life? We all have experienced unique, fascinating moments, no matter how ordinary we feel. You just may not realize you've done neat things. Take a moment now and write out some things you have done. Here are some reminders to get you thinking.

- Where have you traveled?
- What gifts and skills do you have?
- What is different about your family?
- Where did you grow up?
- What sports do you play?

- Have you ever been on TV or in the newspaper?
- Have you met someone famous?
- Ever done a solo somewhere?
- Do you play an instrument, paint, write, or sing?
- Do you know a foreign language?
- How about sign language?
- Ever been on a small plane?
- Have you ever been involved in an emergency situation or rescued someone?
- Have you gotten notoriety for something?
- Have you done something risky?
- Have you done something *really* embarrassing or dumb?
- Where were you when a major event or tragedy happened—9/11, the space-shuttle disaster, an earthquake, tsunami, the Berlin Wall coming down, or some other major events?

Write some of these stories out on your computer or in your journal to remind you of your uniqueness.

Keep in mind that at this stage of the relationship, when it is too fragile to handle serious baggage, you want to interject information about yourself for the purpose of revealing your unique, quirky, charming personality. No sympathy-inducing melodrama. Just be yourself—that is your happy, pleasant-to-be-around self, rather than any "woe is me" side of yourself.

Be His Adoring Fan and Laugh Your Way into His Arms

Laughter is huge on a first date; in fact, during the entire relationship. Men like funny, charming women, not bitter, obnoxious ones. Whatever you do, lean toward the humorous side of life.

Most men love to hear their own voices tell their same stories and repeat their same corny jokes. Let them. Be into his conversation. Your man doesn't have to be Robin Williams, Chris Rock, or Jerry Seinfeld to make you laugh. So cut him some slack and let him entertain you on his level. He needs to know you find him funny when he's trying to be funny. If he deliberately does corny things to impress or entertain you, don't be a snob. Be charmed and laugh with him (not at him). When he tells jokes, laugh. You don't have to fake it and fall off your chair, just show him a twinkle in your eye and an approving smile. If you laugh at his jokes and truly listen to his stories, he will be putty in your hands.

Keep Conversations about Yourself Light and Positive

The first date is not the time to get into your life drama. Talk about what is good in your life. Diminish the bad. If the relationship continues, there will be time for both of you to share the deeper things—after there is enough emotional bond to handle the shock of unpleasant truth. If you've been through an ugly and messy divorce or carry a long list of less-than-happy endings in your personal life, it's better not to let that topic surface for a while. Perhaps you can say, "I haven't made the best choices in men before"; but you don't have to go into every bitter detail of exes who abused, used, or cheated on you.

The Politician in You

Politicians know that just because they are asked a question doesn't mean they have to answer it. Watch any preelection debate or news conference. Politicians are notorious for handling the tough questions in one of two ways. They either answer the question they want to avoid with another question, or they answer a completely different question with such passion and confidence that you somehow are convinced that is the question that was asked in the first place.

This skill takes practice to pull it off, but give it a shot. Next time a date brings up a topic you're not ready to discuss, be a politician. Ask a question back or answer a different one; he may not even notice you're dancing around the subject.

Make Light of Your Pain

If painful topics do come up, and you aren't able to effectively divert the conversation as a slick politician would, then keep it light and try to laugh about it. In the movie *The Holiday*, Cameron Diaz's character is asked if her parents are still together. In reply, she tells about how they were the perfect family, "The Three Musketeers," until she was fifteen, and then one day after school her parents just announced they were getting a divorce. She relays how she'd started laughing because she just knew it was a joke, until she saw her dad's suitcase out of the corner of her eye. She finishes by saying she cried and cried that night, then pulled herself together, and hasn't cried since. She laughs and changes the subject.

This was such a well-written scene. It was an extremely deep, personal, painful moment in her life, yet she managed to spill it, get through it, and move on. Now her date in the movie, played by Jude Law, was sensitive and got the importance of that moment, but he also allowed her to change the subject until another time. So it is possible to reveal a painful experience without turning the night into a melodramatic therapy session that ends up scaring away the second date.

Wash That Heart Off Your Sleeve

Don't wear you heart on your sleeve. You can't. *You* know you're not crazy, but he doesn't. He doesn't need the pressure of "everyone else hurt me, you'd better not" or "my entire happiness depends on your calling me back" or "I just know we are meant to be together, I dreamed of you last night."

Don't blow it by sharing too much right up front. There is no such thing as genuine love at first sight. There is infatuation and attraction at first sight, but it is not sustaining love. It takes time to see whether you have love or lust in common. Keep those hopes and dreams to yourself for now, and enjoy focusing on him.

Don't Freak Him Out

Having differing views is not what prevents second dates. Being of opposing faiths or opposite political parties can be viewed as a challenge or a project for your date. He just may think that is intriguing and want to investigate further or spend time with you to change your views or see if you really are politically savvy.

What *will* scare him away on that first date is telling him you are ready to get married, like right now or soon, or that God told you in a dream last night that you were meeting your husband-to-be tonight. He'll feel you care more about a marriage than getting to know *him*.

Don't advertise that you're looking to get married in the next year or that your biological clock is ticking loudly. In context of the conversation, if it comes up, you can let him know you are interested in getting married when the right one comes along, but don't put pressure on him that you are thinking or hoping he will be that one. It's too soon on a first date.

Show Some Spunk

With all my talk about making the evening all about him and not freaking him out, I'm not saying you have to be sweet, wink, and approve if your date says something inappropriate or offensive or shares views contrary to yours. He may be of an opposite political party or different faith or denomination. He could unknowingly ridicule something or someone you hold dear.

If and when he does offend, respond with how you really feel. Nothing wrong with being real and putting him on the defensive. He is there to win you, and you expect to be treated like a lady. You'll be amazed at how much more he'll respect you for demanding good treatment and how quickly he'll shape up, apologize, and turn on the charm. He only pulls what he can get away with. You don't have to turn into a wicked witch; just expect to be treated like a lady worthy of being pursued, not a one-night disrespected fling or someone thought of as just one of the boys. Get to the point, be firm, and move on. If he says something negative about your denomination or about a handicap or a special interest of yours, contradict him with your view. If your date talks about other attractive women for whatever ridiculous reason, you can say, "Hey, you're not out hanging with the boys, you're with a lady. Check out the other gals when you're with your friends." Sometimes even good guys bring up dumb things just to see how you feel about yourself and if you'll demand to be treated right. They are looking for someone with self-respect not a doormat. They may hang out with a doormat, but they won't pursue or spend money on one.

Being that I was in Hollywood, a town known for its liberal views and lifestyles, it should not surprise you that I had plenty of first dates who held views quite the opposite of mine. They didn't mean to offend me with some of their comments, because they didn't immediately know I held the views they were disrespecting. But I let them know that, as a matter of fact, they were talking about me or mistaking all people associated with that topic as the stereotype. The most polar opposites of me always asked me for a second date—sometimes faster than the others—because I instantly became a challenge or a project of someone for them to change. I must say I took the second dates probably for the same reason, thinking I could change their views. Views were not often changed, but memorable encounters and long-remembered, challenging conversations occurred on both the first and second dates.

People admire spunk. Tell it like it is and stand out rather than remaining silent, polite, and soon to be forgotten.

Automatic Recap

1. Don't blow it at hello. Be on time.
2. Establish consistent, appropriate eye contact throughout

your time together; not a stare or a glare, but focused attention.

3. A great communicator is four people in one—a reporter, politician, psychologist, and fan.

4. The secret formula is found in James 1:19. Be quick to listen, slow to speak, and slow to become angry (or reveal hidden anger).

5. He's the focus, but you can certainly talk about yourself as well; just make it relevant to your conversation and keep it brief.

6. Be brief, witty, and on topic when you speak.

7. If you've got a story you're dying to tell, steer the conversation that way by asking him questions on that topic. When he takes the bait, reel him in.

8. Everyone has stories; reflect on your life and write down your memorable moments—including the happy, sad, scary, adventurous, humorous, and challenging. After you've remembered them, practice telling the stories to your friends in five minutes or less per story. Practice them until you can keep their attention from beginning to end.

9. Be up on the current headlines. This makes you appear knowledgeable of current events, even if you aren't.

10. Think like a reporter. Ask questions; listen to his answers. Ask some more. Just make sure you are listening to his answers rather than worrying about what to ask next.

11. A man loves a woman who laughs at his jokes.

12. It's okay if he notices you're asking a lot of questions. Just let him know you are intrigued with him and want to know more.

13. If painful topics come up, keep your answers light, laugh about it, and change the subject. It's too early in the relation-

ship to share painful feelings. Your date may feel uncomfortable and not call again.

14. Your man does not need to hear you think he may be "the one." He'll surely think you are obsessed with finding a husband, not getting to know him.

15. A first date can handle opposing views and faiths. It cannot handle premature expressions of love.

16. Show some spunk and you'll be remembered. Men love a girl who can speak her mind and be an individual. If you don't agree with his views or the views of someone you are discussing, let him know. Just don't be rude and obnoxious.

Focus on Him

This is a lot to absorb, I know, but once you master the skills of communicating, you'll not only win date after date, you will also improve all your interpersonal relationships. There is a time for everything, and certainly that includes a time to focus on others. Be the interviewer, the psychologist, the politician, and adoring fan; and your phone will ring again. Keeping your date in the spotlight keeps him invested in the evening and tells you what you want to know about him—and that is exactly what you want.

Automatic Journaling

Getting Him at Hello and Beyond

1. Practice the art of making conversation with the person you're speaking to. Today, as you chat with someone, focus on him, his interests, and his perspective on whatever you are discussing. Write about how it went. Consciously do this at least once every single day until it becomes effortless for you.

2. A good listener looks at the person talking, listens to his words, repeats what she thinks was said, and answers with further questions, opinions, or a nod to encourage more. Try this formula on your next face-to-face conversation. How did it go? Did you get it right when you repeated back his or her words? How did you encourage the person to keep talking?

3. Plan out and write a group of questions you think can help you go from casual to serious talk. You're not limited to the one hundred questions listed in this chapter. These are there just to jump-start your creative thinking. Based on your personal ideal-man list, what questions would you begin with, and where will you go from there?

4. Find out what is happening in the world today by checking the daily headlines. Go to the Internet, and visit at least three of these Web sites: www.usatoday.com, www.latimes.com, www.nytimes.com, www.msnbc.com, www.cnn.com, www.people.com, or www.christianitytoday.com. Then visit the Web site of your favorite local TV station or local newspaper (you can search for them on Google). Sign up for at least two daily news alerts.

5. Make a list of ten unique, funny, or intriguing things about

you. This can be a tradition, talent, vacation, hobby, language skill—you name it.

6. Write down five memorable experiences you have lived through thus far. These can be funny or embarrassing, sweet or scary, serious or important. They can be celebrity encounters or moments of notoriety. They can even be participation in a national or worldwide news event. (Look back at the questions I listed on pages 161–62 to spark your memory.)

7. Choose two of the ten unique things or five stories you listed above and turn each into a five-minute story. Then practice reciting these stories to your friends.

8

Let the Sparks Fly!

How to Connect on Date One

irector Rob Reiner's classic date movie *When Harry Met Sally* made Billy Crystal and Meg Ryan household names. We fell in love with Meg Ryan for her portrayal of a spunky Sally Albright and Billy Crystal for his portrayal of Harry Burns with his wacky view of male/female relationships. What I cherish most about this film is the charming montage at the end of the film as the credits are rolling. Before an interview with movie couple Harry and Sally, director Rob Reiner has real-life couples married fifty years or longer share insights to their longevity. I sit through each interview every time I watch the film; it is just precious. They finish each other's sentences. They move at the same pace. They sit in the same position. They almost seem like clones of each other.

Ah, love . . . When two souls connect with just the right spark, they seem to almost merge into one person. At least that's the way it appears when you track some celebrities' history of love. Take Brad Pitt for instance. He seems to take on the physical appearance of all his loves—from hair color to fashion statement— tracking all the way back from Juliette Lewis to Gwyneth Paltrow, Jennifer Aniston to Angelina Jolie. Not all of us are this extreme, but as we spend time with someone, we tend to adopt some of his style, mannerisms, and moods. Think about those couples who have been married for fifty years.

How can you jump-start this potential fifty-year connection process on the very first date and go from nothing in common to kindred spirits? How can you progress from perfect strangers to soul mates, even if you haven't yet perfected the art of conversation? Simple. Just follows these secrets. In this chapter I'm going to teach you five fun skills you can develop—all without taking a class or going to school. You'll learn how to *"mirror"* your date to make him feel comfortable and in sync with you; you'll discover that *flattery*, my darling, will get you everywhere if used genuinely and in the right dosage; and that *laughter* can bond the two of you together in a special way. Plus, I'll tell you how to make romantic contact through *touch*, with a smooth brush of your hand across his arm at just the right moment; and finally, I'll teach you how to combine all these bonding secrets by *gazing* into his eyes without freaking him out. Master this chapter, and you'll connect with your man on a subconscious level—and you will rarely find yourself without a second date.

The Magic of Mirroring

American Idol host Ryan Seacrest knows how to effortlessly connect with whomever he is with. Notice his demeanor the next time you see him on camera. Whether he's talking to a contestant, a co-host, or an interviewee, he assumes their energy. If they are hyper, he becomes hyper; if they jump, he jumps; if they are mellow, he becomes mellow; if they frown, he frowns. I don't know if he even realizes he's doing it; he's just so in the moment and focused on the guest that he instantly bonds with them, and we get great television.

This powerful yet little-known secret, which Ryan Seacrest automatically performs, is called *mirroring*. I first heard of mirroring when I was just beginning to succeed at dating in my early twenties. I had discovered this little book on how to make a man fall in love with you. I was so embarrassed I owned it that I kept a black book cover over it and hid it under my bed—honestly. Some of the secrets were silly and manipulative, almost like casting a spell on the guy to get him to keep calling you.

The unrealistic part of this author's method is that she expected you to keep this game going forever. You were not free to be yourself, because the guy fell in love with the "actress" and was calling back that character, not the unseen real you. What's wrong with that? Besides everything, she was advocating role-playing—being someone you're not. Maybe doing that for a date or two wouldn't be the end of the world; but keeping it up forever gets old and frankly is not fair to either of you. He doesn't know the real you, thus he doesn't love the real you. Ultimately both you and your date will lose.

Rather than being an imposter trying to be something you're not, I'm advocating you commit to stop being self-absorbed (no offense, we're all guilty of self-absorption at times) for at least the first two dates, and instead put your attention and focus all on your date so you can get in tune with who he is.

And mirroring was indeed the gem I took away from that book, which helped me almost immediately get in tune with my dates. It was the first time I'd heard of this secret but not the last. And mirroring works in *any* human interaction, as Ryan Seacrest and other great interviewers prove. I've since used it in business, television interviews, and basically all my interpersonal relationships. People are just more comfortable around people who are like them. The familiar brings trust and comfort; the unfamiliar brings fear and distrust.

Mirroring your date will entice him to ask you for that second date and will definitely help in your mission to get him to fall madly in love with you. How do you mirror him? You do it by jumping on his wavelength, assuming his vibe—in other words, you become his mirrored reflection.

From the very first meeting, not to mention first date, mirror back to him what he puts out to you with his body language, his tone of voice, his movement, his demeanor, and his gestures. You want him to feel comfortable with you, as though you are meant to be together. How much, how long, and how discreet do you need to be? Go for smooth transitions. You are not playing an annoying game of copycat that is obvious and disconcerting. You are allowing him to settle into whatever moment he is in and following suit in a casual readjustment. You want to get in sync with him like you do when you start moving to the beat of a melody.

For example, if it suddenly occurs to you that you are leaning forward on your chair and he is completely relaxed, almost reclining in his, take a breath and slowly assume a similarly relaxed position. If he changes positions to the edge of his seat, you will too, in a few moments. None of your changes are abrupt. You're just keeping up with his mood, tone, and movements. Think of it as going on a walk. If you're walking next to each other, you have to be walking at the same pace. If he speeds up, you speed up, if he slows down, you slow down. He will not be offended and say you are just copying him if you keep pace with him on the walk.

That is what mirroring is—keeping up with your man. Same tone, same general movements and position and energy. So you're sitting at the dinner table and your date puts his elbows on the table. Do the same. If he takes a drink of his beverage, you take a drink of yours. If he leans back, relaxed in his chair, within a few moments, do the same. Mirror the vibe he puts out. If he is relaxed, relax. If he is animated, wake up and be animated. If he is using a loud voice and rapid words, raise your voice to a similar volume and speed. If he is whispering, don't talk in a loud or even normal voice—whisper. Mirroring happens all the time and, often, subconsciously rather than deliberately. It's almost automatic when you connect with each other. That is what happens when you have joined each other's wavelength or are so engrossed in the moment you just seem to be on the same rhythm.

The sole purpose of mirroring is for your date to feel as if you two are made for each other. You have much in common, and he wants to keep spending time with you.

Prior to his megafame as a talk show host, Dr. Phil McGraw was a successful trial consultant who prepared witnesses to be effective on the stand before a jury. His research showed that jurors are more likely to believe witnesses who are like them. Dr. Phil would train his witnesses to make eye contact and, thus, connect with jurors who were the most like them (similar backgrounds, lifestyles, or jobs). "You don't pander to them; you just connect with them. This is genuine and real, not coming from a place of manipulation."[1]

The same technique works on a first date. Your first dates are hopefully never as intense as a courtroom drama; however, if finding common ground through a look, gesture, or stance can help in a courtroom, certainly it can work in a more relaxed environment. Spend that first date finding your similarities, and your date will come back for more.

Before you try mirroring on your man, practice by mirroring your friends and family members. Then try it in your work environment and when you are trying to persuade someone to do what you want. Does it work? Do you find people more agreeable to your requests? Does anyone comment on your movements? The more you practice, the better you'll get, and the more likely no one will know when you're doing it. Rather, they'll just be more relaxed around you and, thus, enjoy hanging around you.

You can even practice mirroring during the flirting phase, when you're trying to get that first date. Watch your man across the room and mirror his movements. But remember, you're not playing copycat; you are watching and slowly adjusting to his posture. Stand up, sit down, lean forward, lean back, just not immediately after he does.

Physical mirroring involves more than just stance, hand gestures, and sitting position. You are also mimicking his volume and speed of speech, his energy level, and his pacing. I am by nature a fast-talking, hyper gal. That works great in Los Angeles, New York, and Chicago. But in most other places, folks prefer a slightly slower speed. As a speaker, I've had to learn to assume a talking pace that is comfortable for my audience. You are basically doing the same thing on a first date. You pick up on the pace of your man and assume it as your own.

Dr. Tracy Cabot believes you can be honest with yourself and still agree with a man over anything. If you hate sports, but he loves sports, mirror him by saying, "You like sports." Bingo, you've just mirrored his preference without having to mirror his love for the activity. "Just getting into agreement with him and then beginning to mirror his belief systems can make him trust you the way a patient trusts a doctor," Cabot says. She says there are no limits to the areas in which you can mirror him; just let your imagination run wild. "Mirror the rhythm of [his] sentences, the blinking of his eyes, the way he views his universe, his breathing. . . . He'll be putty in your hands."[2]

Listen to your date and latch on to anything that matches you. But be sincere in your efforts. If you tell lies about your similarities, it will come out eventually. You don't have to be identical. If he likes chocolate ice cream and you like strawberry ice cream, don't swear chocolate is your favorite flavor. Find a way to bring those two flavors together. You can say, "Hey, we both like basic flavors rather than the fancy exotics." See, you've established common ground. He could love baseball and you may not even know what a bat looks like, but you have a relative who played. Great, share that. You've validated him again.

On your first date, you are helping yourself out by making mirroring deliberate until it is natural. You're just paying attention and making it happen—if you haven't already automatically mirrored each other.

Flattery, My Darling, Will Get You Everywhere!

Girls, here's an important insight into the heart of a man that far too few women appear to realize—men need admiration! Male or female, we all yearn to be looked up to; we're all insecure and need that praise. Besides, it's a commodity in too short supply in this world. But men . . . they crave it. They love it, though they'll say they don't. Just don't make your flattery the stereotypical stuff they hear all the time. Be original.

Smart, magnetic women know how to meet the male need for validation by tuning in and appreciating their date for exactly what he wants to be appreciated. So pay attention to your man and pick up the clues concerning what he is most proud of—it may be his job, his car, his watch, his education, his discipline, his hair, his muscles, anything. He'll talk about what matters to him, or he'll point it out more than once, or you won't be able to miss it because it's spit-shined so bright it shouts, "Notice me, notice me!" (such as his car or other prized possession). A magnetic woman notices and listens to her date and sees rather quickly what matters.

Few things will win your man's heart more quickly than genuine, specific flattery. For flattery to work in your favor, *you* have to believe what you say and *he* has to believe you mean it. Flatter him with believable, coveted praise, rather than superficial, generic words. Everyone is positively affected by genuine flattery and will keep coming back for more, but insincere praise is a turnoff. Master the skill of sincere flattery, and you will rarely find yourself without an automatic second date.

Here's a list to give you ideas of what to compliment: you can flatter your man's accomplishments, accolades, confidence, presence, memory, wit, mind, laugh, smile, cooking, cleanliness, classiness, creativity, dedication, talent, looks, physique, teeth, lips, eyes, height, shoulders, muscles, hair, cologne, clothes, tie, jacket, shoes, hat, rings, watch, sunglasses, bravery, strength, accessories, fashion, and decorating taste. You can admire something he's written, said, sung, drawn, painted, or memorized. The list goes on and on. You can flatter him about any of these things and more—but only if they are true.

If you know his first and last name and want to find some interesting scoop on your date ahead of time, go online and Google his name to see if anything comes up. Not everyone has an online presence, but if he's accomplished much in his profession, college, or anything that hit the media, it will appear. Then you'll know where to steer the conversation so you can praise him for those accomplishments.

When you flatter him, describe the details. Rather than, "You've got great eyes," say, "I love that shade of green." Instead of, "I like your car," say, "I'm so impressed with how meticulous and shiny this car is." Rather than saying, "You are so handsome," say, "I've never seen such a chiseled jawline; I like it!" Instead of, "How do you know that stuff? I am so impressed," say, "I cannot believe you calculated those numbers in your head; I could never do that." Do you see the difference? Superficial, general compliments will come across as insincere and turn your date off. It's better to take the time to come up with something specific, even something like he has neat eyebrows, if you can't think of anything else. Say that and he'll think, *Wow, she notices the details.*

Don't overpower and freak him out by overdoing it, though. If he has achieved tons of awards for his medical research, certainly let him know you admire his brain and contribution to society. But don't gush on and on about it. If you do, he'll either not believe you or he'll fear that you're a soon-to-be stalker, falling for his image not his person. Be creative. If it's genuine and heartfelt, he will eat it up. But do it in small doses.

I remember the first time I met Bruce Willis. He was just becoming a star, but not yet a superstar. We were backstage at the Emmy Awards, and I knew he wasn't needed on stage for a bit. He was quite single at the time, and I was dressed to kill, so I figured I had a shot at romance. But I blew it.

I went up to him with way too big a grin and way too much energy and announced "I love, love, *love* your show. You will be a huge star!"

He just looked at me and sarcastically said, "Wow, thanks."

Oops, overkill. I got the message and walked away.

Men who are high profile have their egos fed with praise constantly. If your guy falls in this category, you'll have to be even more creative. You don't want to say the same things he hears every day. If you offer too much adulation, he'll consider you a fan rather than an equal.

By the time I had my Bruce Willis fiasco, about a year after my Billy Crystal encounter, I had learned my lesson. The next time I was thrust side by side with a superstar who intrigued me, I composed myself and acted normal.

It happened five months later at the Grammy Awards. I was able to hang out on the set during rehearsals as well as the day of the show. During rehearsals I happened to end up sitting next to Paul Stanley, the lead singer of the rock group KISS. After chitchatting a bit about the show and what they were scheduled to do, I began inquiring about his career path and admiring his ability to stay on top of such a competitive business for such a long time (notice I admired him as a peer—not as a starstruck fan). I was genuinely engrossed in his stories of how he got to where he was and how much marketing and business savvy he and his partner, Gene Simmons, had. The conversation flowed naturally. By the day of the show, he asked for my number, and a few weeks later he actually called from the road. When my receptionist announced he was on the phone, I was rather pleasantly surprised. You can get *your* man to respond equally well to your flattery. Just be normal, genuine, and generous—without being excessive.

By the way, don't make your compliments overly sexual. You are not using flattery to come on to him; you're using it as a tool to bond with his heart and meet his needs. If you make it sexual, it's just about lust and not about his person.

Remember, you're a self-assured, magnetic woman who notices and listens to her man. Be impressed with what you hear and see, and tell him about it. If you'll admire him, you will have

met one of his deepest needs, and before you know it, he'll be
back for more.

Laughter Is Still the Best Medicine

Have you ever noticed that when you try to tell someone about a
hilarious moment that left you in tears, it just doesn't deliver the
same punch to others as it did for the people present when it
happened? You know, the ol' "I guess you had to be there" syn-
drome. Laughter has a way of bonding people through a special
moment-in-time shared exclusively. Everyone can use more humor in his or her life, and certainly that includes everyone on a
first date. Bring laughter to your date.

If you have a hard time laughing at your life or if you've been
accused of being horrible at telling stories, go out right now and
buy a copy of *Stand-Up Comedy: The Book* by Judy Carter or
another book on doing comedy. You don't have to start showing
up at open-mike nights; just learn how to improve your wit.
Carter's book is great because she has you write out many of your
life experiences (the good, the bad, and the awful), and then she
teaches you how to turn them into laughter. This will certainly
come in handy with someone new. Why not tell your new man
about your life and leave him in stitches?

Make it a goal for you and your new man to laugh. When you
are amused, laugh. When you're embarrassed, laugh. When
you're frustrated, laugh. If everything goes wrong, laugh. Emotionally, believe it or not, laughter and tears are closely related.
The important difference is that tears leave you vulnerable, risking feelings of "too close too soon," especially on a first date.
Laughter, on the other hand, is safe and welcome, leaving him
wanting more. Laughter is not only good for the soul, it's great

for getting your man to keep on coming back! So lighten up and discover your inner comedian, and your date will leave feeling, *Wow, she just makes me feel good!*

Reach Out and Touch

Okay now, you are ready to mirror your man's body language, and you've learned how to make him laugh. What more can you do? We're almost there. There are a few more secrets to help reel him in. One way to get your man to bond with you is through touch. I'm not talking a major seduction here. I'm talking brushing your hand or fingers across his hand, arm, back, knee, or finger tips. You want to make your touch seem like it's part of your normal hand gestures as if you're saying, "I know," "I so agree," "I understand," or "I feel that way too."

Let's say you're talking over dinner. Here are a couple of examples: If you're telling a story and you want to emphasize a point, you can reach over and touch his hand (or his forearm if he's holding his fork) while you say, "And you know what . . . ," or "Oh, I meant to tell you . . ." Or you can say something like, "You mentioned you like golf, so you'll love this story." Right when you say "You mentioned . . . ," reach over and touch his hand (or forearm) for a moment, perhaps leave it there a second or two, then draw your hand back to where it was and continue talking. That little touch bonds you together like, "Hey, this is between you and me, not the crowd surrounding us." It's also a good move when you're in a crowd or on a group date, because it reminds the two of you that you are together. It's not pushy; rather it plays to his subconscious. If done well and several times over the course of the date, the subtle impact of your touch will make a lasting impression.

Remember the book I told you about that first taught me the magic of mirroring? Well, this book also touted anchoring his love by making sure you touch him every time he has a smile on his face or is sharing a happy memory, so that subconsciously he will associate those happy feelings with you. I tried that method, and it always felt manufactured and unnatural to me. Make your touch be about sharing moments and connecting rather than about casting some spell of transference; otherwise, you make the date about manipulation rather than having a good time and getting to know someone.

Casual touch can also be a way to imply you like your date without being forward. You are not kissing him. You are merely making skin-to-skin contact in a nonaggressive manner to help you connect.

Touch can show protectiveness, such as when a man politely touches his date on the back as they walk, letting others know, "She is with me right now, and I am protecting her."

One of the most romantic moments in *The Holiday* was when Jude Law's daughters tell the Cameron Diaz character that their family pet name is the Three Musketeers, the same name her family used to have. Upon the little girl's announcement, we see Jude Law's character discreetly reach over and touch Cameron Diaz's finger tips with his—a touch that spoke volumes without his saying a word. His touch let her know he understood how she felt at that moment and was there for her.

Gaze into His Eyes

Eye contact, eye contact, eye contact. I guess the reason I keep repeating this one is that I want you to remember it. Mirroring, flattery, laughter, and touch are all powerful tools for helping your man fall for you. However, if you want to take it to the next level, make sure all these bonding secrets are combined with plenty of gazing into the eyes. Direct eye contract is your emotionally charged clincher for drawing your man in. You see, it's safe and noncommittal to look at his hands or his face, anywhere but into the window to his soul. You make it personal when you gaze into his eyes.

As reported in a recent issue of *New Scientist* magazine, dating experts and flirts know that eye contact is an emotionally loaded act. Psychologists now agree there is an igniting power at the meeting of the eyes. "When pairs of strangers were asked to gaze into each other's eyes, it was perhaps not surprising that their feelings of closeness and attraction rocketed compared with, say, gazing at each other's hands. More surprising was that a couple in one such experiment ended up getting married. Neuroscientists have shed some light on what's going on: meeting another person's gaze lights up brain regions associated with rewards. The bottom line is that eye contact can work wonders, but make sure you get your technique right: if your gaze isn't reciprocated, you risk coming across as a stalker."[3]

So take it from the experts, be it flirts, jury consultants, or psychologists—look your man in the eye, and pay attention when he talks to you. Few things make a person feel more appreciated, valued, and trusted than the courtesy of undivided attention.

Automatic Recap

1. Mirror his movements, posture, demeanor, and gestures.
2. Mirror the volume, speed, and tone of his voice.
3. Your man may notice you are mirroring him; but if you do it

smoothly, he won't think it is deliberate, and he certainly won't mind.

4. When you mirror someone, you cause him to feel liked and validated.
5. Men need and crave admiration.
6. Flattery, my darling, will get you everywhere, because no one can resist heartfelt praise.
7. When flattering, skip the generalization and get specific; it will be perceived as sincere.
8. Laughter truly is the best medicine. Bring humor and laughter into your evening.
9. Read a book or take a class on stand-up comedy to bring out your wit and charm.
10. When all else fails, laugh.
11. Connect with your man with a light touch on the arm.
12. Casual, nonsexual touch is a nonthreatening way to shift the mood from platonic to romantic.
13. Gazing into his eyes will make him feel as appreciated as flattery.

The Five Connectors

The Bible says three strands woven together are not easily broken. Weave together all five of the connectors we talked about in this chapter and, wow, your man is a goner! You have jumped onto the same page. You can be the most perfect girl in the world for that bachelor, but if you don't let him in on your similarities, he will be clueless. So spend those first two dates convincing him of your alikeness. Even if you have to search long and hard for sameness, make the effort. Master these skills, and it will be as easy as leaning forward and leaning back.

You no longer have to panic if you begin your date seeming to have nothing in common. Practice these techniques—mirroring, flattery, laughter, touch, and gazing into his eyes—and you can go from perfect strangers to kindred spirits in a matter of one date. Just jump on his wavelength and assume his vibe.

Automatic Journaling
Practicing Your Jumpstart

1. Practice your mirroring skills. Without announcing it, mirror several people today. Mirror the stance, sitting positions, tone of voice, and speed of speaking. Did they notice? If they didn't, you don't have to tell them now. Just keep it up. If they noticed, you just need more practice. Write down how it went.

2. When you are talking to someone today, lower your voice to almost a whisper. Did they begin speaking at the same volume?

3. Practice agreeing with others. As you talk to someone today, honestly agree with something he says. If he says something you don't agree with, find something about it to agree on and point that out—e.g., if he likes chocolate ice cream and you like strawberry, agree that you both like classic flavors. If he loves baseball and you don't, you can agree that pro-baseball players are great athletes, etc. Get creative and write down how you did.

4. Make flattery a part of your life. Begin pointing out things you admire and like about others. Be as specific as you can but don't overdo it. If you practice on others often enough, it will become automatic for you to notice what to compliment. Find at least one thing to compliment about the next ten people you talk to this week.

5. Practice researching people on the Internet. Go to www .google.com and search for your name. Does anything come up? Click on some of the things that appear and see if they

are indeed about you. Now type in a few people you know. What comes up about them?

6. Write down a time you blew it on a date by being insincere or overenthusiastic in your flattery. How could you have flattered more effectively?

7. Write out one of your embarrassing or sad moments. How can you turn that into a humorous story? If you have trouble doing so, pick up a book or take a class on stand-up comedy, and learn to laugh at yourself and your life. Pick Judy Carter's book *Stand-Up Comedy* for help on your humor.

To Kiss or Not to Kiss

How to Say Goodnight

just love the movie *Never Been Kissed*, starring Drew
Barrymore and Michael Vartan, that cute guy from *Alias*. I so
relate to the torment Josie Geller (Barrymore's character)
felt during her ugly-duckling high-school years. If you've yet to
experience that one memorable moment of a "meaningful" first
kiss or if you just want to reminisce—rent that film!

My first kiss was not exactly as special as Josie Geller's, as she
stood on the pitcher's mound in front of a stadium filled with
scores of cheering fans and news cameras. Mine was more sub-
dued and private but just as memorable to me. I was twelve and
"in love" with the preacher's kid. My girlfriend felt the same
about my brother, so we did what controlling young girls do—we
set up a game of Truth or Dare among the four of us. We girls

prearranged what we would ask and dare. When my guy finally chose a dare (he kept asking for "truth" over "dare"—ugh!), he was dared to French kiss me. I was so excited.

A long, now humorous, story made short, the less-than-perfect first kiss left that twelve-year-old girl thinking that this boy and I would be in love forever. Wrong! Rude awakening came the next day as my girlfriend and I were on our way to the store to buy some candy. We ran into my brother and that boy, who were also on a candy run. When my brother saw his gal, he greeted her warmly, grabbed her hand, and they strolled off together. With a beaming smile and hope in my heart, I walked up to my boy, expecting the same. What I got instead was, "What do you want? I don't like you, and don't expect me to hold your hand!" Ouch, my first blatant rejection! I was devastated. My girlfriend saw the whole thing and came back to console me. We continued the candy trip on ahead of the boys, but life as I knew it was never the same.

How about you? Did your first kiss go better? Was it everything you dreamed it would be, or did it leave you hoping the next kiss would offer future romance? I learned a lot from my first encounter, and much of it has been reinforced by science and society over the years that have followed. I learned two things in particular.

First, getting physical does not mean the same thing to a boy that it does to a girl. I learned this at twelve and have seen it proven time and time again, not just through my personal experience but by observation of others and research by experts. Just because he will gladly kiss you (or more), doesn't mean he has feelings for you. Males are just wired differently than females. The cliché that men offer love for sex and women offer sex for love is true. The physical and the emotional are compartmentalized for men and are usually merged for women.

The second thing I learned from my first kiss was that the cloud-nine emotions you feel in anticipation of and during a kiss are not indicative of the longevity of the relationship or even proof of your own genuine feelings of love. That feeling of elation is a chemical reaction from your electrifying lip-lock. It is not an enduring phenomenon.

First-date kisses—in fact, first kisses with any new man in your life—are emotionally charged events. They not only release a mystery chemical that makes us feel those gushy "in love" feelings, but they also take us back to our naive first kiss and the hope for a budding romance that we read into that embrace.

In this chapter, I'm going to walk you through those good-bye moments at the end of first dates and show you how to become a sweet memory etched in his mind. We look at several variations of your approach, delivery, and closure for that perfect first good-bye. By planning potential scenarios ahead of time, you will automatically ease your anxiety over what often comprises the most awkward moment of the evening. How's that for magnetism?

What will you do if he moves in for your lips? Do you kiss or not kiss? And *if* you are thinking about letting your lips connect at good-bye, what kind of kiss and for how long? Should you close the door to any serious embrace by initiating a peck on his cheek or lips with a quick, "I've had a nice time, bye"? Or do you allow him to make the moves and open yourself up to his embrace or possibly more? Or do you hold back and make him long for the hope of that first passionate embrace on a future date? How much is just enough to whet his appetite, and how much risks rejection or worse, a silence that screams, "What do you want? I don't like you"?

Can a passionate kiss, a soft meeting of the lips, a lingering hug, or even just a meaningful gaze be enough to etch you on his mind and guarantee you a second date? Yes it can. It's all in your approach, delivery, and close. And as a self-confident, self-controlled, magnetic woman, your personal combination of those three is up to you.

What He's Really Thinking

Before I deal with all those front-door dilemmas and talk about your approach, delivery, and close, I want to share with you a few things about how men really think. I know you probably already know this, but let's go over it anyway. I specifically want to talk about how men think about the physical connection.

Since men and women are so different in their thinking, having a real understanding of those differences can save you a lot of unnecessary heartache. So hang on while we look at the meaning and dynamics of a typical male's attraction and physical advances.

Passion and Interest Are *Not* the Same Thing

Dr. John Gray (author of *Men Are from Mars, Women Are from Venus*) warns that a man's initial attraction "has nothing to do with who this woman is, nor does it reflect a willingness or desire to know her or have a relationship with her. He only wants to see more, touch more, and feel more."[1] And those feelings of wanting more of you are just for the moment and often forgotten as soon as he falls asleep.

Huge, gigantic, eye-opening lesson here, so don't miss this: even if he kisses you, caresses you, or more, this in no way means he has emotional feelings for you! Men are often able to compartmentalize their emotions and separate them from their physical attractions. Passion and interest are not necessarily the same thing.

I'm not saying whether it's a good or a bad idea to kiss on a first date. I've kissed on the lips perhaps as often as I've hugged and politely kissed on the cheek. But remember, whatever you do with your man on a first date, he will absolutely, unequivocally assume you do this with every other guy you go out with! Forget the "I've never done this before," even if it's true, because he won't believe you.

He Likes a Challenge

Remember, I've said these secrets work on all men—the good, the bad, and the ugly. They work on reformed womanizers too. And I'm telling you that "not putting out" to a known womanizer will get him pursuing you so fast he won't know what hit him. Mr. Smooth Talker is not used to "no." He won't stop thinking about you, because you are different from the other women in his life. You have self-respect. Rather than being a tease, you have become his challenge. He'll want you.

Legendary movie star Warren Beatty used to be one of the many rumored womanizers in Hollywood. He dated most every starlet to grace Tinseltown, including Goldie Hawn, Candice Bergen, Joan Collins, Brigitte Bardot, Diane Keaton, Elle Macpherson, Cher, Madonna, and Carly Simon (who is rumored to have written "You're So Vain" about him). Yet for decades no woman could get him to commit. That was, until a gorgeous, self-respecting actress by the name of Annette Bening captured his heart by playing hard to get. He went after her until she was his, and the notorious actor finally settled down and got married. Bening maintained self-respect and said no, over and over, and she captured the heart of the noncommittal, unattainable bachelor.

I've been out with good boys and bad boys, shy guys and funny guys, famous men and unknown men. And one thing is consistent with all of them: getting that second date is not about putting out: it's about holding back—not just in your words and your neediness—but also holding back your passion. Of course, getting that second date involves physical chemistry and attraction, but what makes it automatic is a powerful mental connection mixed with the adrenaline of a challenge.

The physical is the mindless part of a man, not the logical thinking part. And it's that thinking side of a man that compels him to call you again. The physical attraction is in the moment and subsides the moment you leave his side. Thought lingers. Want to be a challenge and get under his skin? Less is more, especially on a first date. You definitely want to leave him wanting more of you so he can think about you. With a smirk on his face, you want him to reminisce on everything that was said and done during your time together, not just the forgettable good-bye. (I know, I know. To you, the good-bye is never forgettable; but we're talking men here, and they are chemically different from us.) Bottom line, when your first get-together concludes, you want that good-bye to bring him back for more of you, no matter if your good-bye is a wave, gaze, peck, kiss, or more.

There are plenty of smooth talkers on a mission for one thing from you—and it's not a stroll in the park. If he gets angry when you say no, he is not interested in your mind nor will he be spending time and money on you in the future, *whether you give in or not*. His anger reveals he is not looking for a relationship; he is looking for casual, no-obligation sex. Not only is there little guarantee for a second date with this kind of guy, he may not even remember your name in the morning.

On the other hand, if you say no to your date's excessive advances, you have just etched your memory on his brain. If he has any redeeming quality to his character, you'll be getting a callback in a flash. If he doesn't call back, then he is a loser. Let it go!

At risk of becoming redundant, let me repeat: if you put out you may get another call, but not an early-in-the-week phone call to book you before you get busy. You risk a last-minute, late-night call for you to just come on over. That is not a date; it's a hookup. You're on the road to a secret fling not an open relationship. And a magnetic woman always deserves better!

Being Easy Won't Catch Him

Most women are just wired with the desire to please their man. And we're often under the mistaken impression that the way to a man's heart is through his bed—even though our grandmas told us it's through his stomach! And as we've been saying, most guys are wired to take advantage of our desire to please—because they want to be pleased, physically!

When we give in to his advances for more—whether we are physically into it too or just want to please him—we'll discover that the surest way to lose his heart is to allow the physical to take the lead. Guys like and remember a challenge—no matter what they say in the heat of the moment.

But I Just Want to Please Him

A frequent reason women give in to a date's physical advances is because she is insecure and wants to *please* her man. She fears "no" will upset and in turn scare him away. And a lot of guys know just how to play off this fear. More than once I've heard a pouting date's response, "I'm not mad, I'm just disappointed," as he got shut down and sent home. A smart girl sees through this charade, puts on the brakes, and ushers her date sweetly out the door. Otherwise, she'll discover the hard way that pleasing his impulsive urges won't keep him; instead, she'll be left alone, dumbfounded and bitter.

Insecure women are natural people pleasers. I know that full well, as I am a certified recovering people pleaser myself. Saying no and having boundaries on a date may be uncomfortable for the moment, but it is crucial to your self-respect and self-love. Taking the people-pleasing easy route of saying yes to (or just going along with) excessive physical touch carries no obligation for your man to call back after his passion of the moment has subsided and he's back to his normal life. And it is in his normal life, after you're gone, that he decides whether or not to call.

If you want to be remembered, it won't be because you were great in bed. Hopping into bed is the easiest way to be forgotten. So what makes a man come back for more? Dr. John Gray says that "one key to being remembered is, in fact, the *opposite* of what many women think. A woman mistakenly assumes that if she is eager to please a man, he will be pleased and become more interested. Yes, he will be pleased, but he will not necessarily become more actively interested.[2]

He Cried "More, More, More!"

Men are not the only ones who get physically excited. We women have hormones too! And we, too, can get caught up in the physical sensations of the moment. But as magnetic women looking for a second date and even the hope of a long-term relationship, we have to keep our heads about us.

One problem with throwing caution to the wind is that once the physical has begun, it always progresses for both the man and the woman. What satisfies today is rarely enough for tomorrow. "More, more, more!" is an accurate description of lust. Once you do something a few times, it's pretty hard to prevent wanting more and going further. If from the start you give in to lust and you are given opportunities to keep seeing each other, you'll probably become addicted to one another's bodies, but not your minds and souls. Sex never equals commitment, to a man. Ladies you have got to wake up and get that in your head. Being easy won't catch him.

The Surest Way to Lose His Heart

Going overboard physically almost guarantees that you'll lose exactly what you're after—his heart. When you allow physical attraction to take over, you put a stop to open communication, and it's no longer about the whole package. And that whole package is what a man requires to allow himself to follow his heart.

What makes the physical side so confusing to women is that men are so good at making us feel special when they caress and kiss. They make you feel as if you are the only one. Heck, many men even say those words when they're swept up in the mindless moments of attraction. You cannot believe a man's words spoken in a moment of passion—*especially, unequivocally, definitely not on a first date*. If he is telling you no one has ever made him feel this way and it is your first date, you must understand it is his passion speaking, not his heart.

Dr. John Gray warns ladies of this very thing: "A woman must remember that she is not that special," Gray says, "because there are a lot of women to whom a man can feel physically attracted. It is a good beginning, but it doesn't necessarily mean anything more."[3] The man is caught up in good feelings of the moment.

He may temporarily be convinced that you are the absolute woman of his dreams. "In this case, he may believe and behave as though he were in love with who [you] are, but only time will tell."[4]

Gray goes on to say that there are other powerful elements of chemistry that have to be there for the man to pursue you further, such as potential for friendship and a mental attraction. If you allow the physical to take precedence, especially in the beginning of your relationship, and a first date is certainly the *beginning*, the other elements of chemistry are not allowed to develop. Attraction soon fades or grows cold, and you soon slip from his mind.

Getting physical changes the whole dynamic of the relationship. It's like you're saying, *Hey, I don't know you and I don't know if we have what it takes for forever or even tomorrow; but it feels good, so who cares. Let's shut down our minds and throw inhibitions to the wind.* If you adopt that careless attitude, you've done both of you a huge disservice, because you've cheapened your relationship before it starts. You are definitely no longer a challenge (which men prefer), and you've put all kinds of roadblocks in your pathway to his heart. Giving you his heart takes more than a few hours. In fact, it takes time—days, weeks, or months—for a man to grow to love you from the inside out—and that, by the way, is the only way a man will commit.

Decide Before You Go

Okay, okay, I've made my point. Now that you have an idea of how a man thinks and understand that being easy really won't catch him, how far *will* you go on a first date? Whatever you decide, you'll have to make that decision *before* that first date. If you wait until you're at the door, you are in danger of either stumbling through the whole closing—when a little planning can allow it to be so nice!—or you'll go farther than you want to go, because in the heat of the moment you'll lose your head. Decide before you go.

Will your boundaries be that you not touch on the lips on a first date? If that's your decision, how will you initiate the good-bye to maintain that limit? Will you offer your hand for a shake? Step forward and initiate a good-bye hug, then wave as you walk inside, or just give him a no-contact smile?

Will you prefer to say good-bye with a sweet kiss on the cheek? That will mean one of two things, either you'll be turning your cheek toward his face as he moves in for the kiss, or you'll initiate the kiss yourself and move in to kiss him on his cheek. What are you going to do?

Will you allow him to move in for a soft kiss on the lips? Or do you prefer to initiate that kiss to maintain control of the brevity and intensity of the moment?

When you want to maintain the above kinds of control, it can be appropriate for you to initiate the good-bye. But if you want more than a peck, leave it to the man to make the moves; then you can put on the brakes if and when he attempts to push past your limits.

You may be comfortable kissing and embracing or even "making out" for five minutes or thirty minutes or more. But that doesn't mean your date has the same restraint to keep it at just hugs and kisses. So be aware that once his personal line of self-control is crossed, you may have unleashed a monster and be stuck with the not-fun task of shutting him down.

Boundary Decisions

A magnetic woman feels good about herself and her actions. And to keep feeling good about herself, she has to know how to set boundaries and how to keep them. A great guideline for determining your personal boundaries when it comes to passion is not to do anything with your date tonight that might make you feel like you need to apologize tomorrow. If you've caught yourself saying to a date (true or not true), "I've never done this before," then most likely you've violated your own moral code and perhaps even his.

I love author Josh McDowell's definition of dating success: Rather than success meaning to "score," he calls success (and I especially emphasize this as success on a first date) as having "an absence of guilt and a good positive feeling about your date, yourself, God and your future."[5]

He's Depending on You

Whatever boundaries you decide on, go into the date knowing that *you* have to be in charge of the physical limits if you want to see him again. Like it or not, most men are just not strong enough to be in charge of the physical arena—even nice, Christian boys can get carried away on a first date if the moon is full, Sirius Satellite Radio is tuned in, and your fragrance melts his inhibitions. Watch out; you're toast. A man will categorize you by how you respond to his advances. If you weaken, going well beyond kissing on that first date, he will not keep you in the angelic-lady category. Get what I'm saying?

When it comes to magnetic women, men are weak. It's flattering to be able to affect a man that way; however, the ability comes with a price. Along with his weakness for you comes a crumbling of his inhibitions, followed by an unfair assessment as he thinks back on the evening. You will be blamed if *his* internal value boundary is crossed by how far the two of you go—and he won't tell you that. Hey, Adam did the same thing in the Garden of Eden. He blamed Eve for making him take a bite of that forbidden fruit. "The woman you put here with me—she gave me some fruit from the tree, and I ate it."[6] Read the entire chapter of Genesis 3.

Just because he acts a certain way does not mean he approves of his own actions. Being human, he will look for someone else to blame. You're there too, so it will be your fault. He may have pushed you to go further than you wanted. It may have been all his doing, but you gave in, so you're to blame. Yes, it's a double standard, but that is just the way it is.

You must be the strong one. Just put on the brakes before passion takes over your own ability to reason. You've got to make certain the physical goes slow before it all goes downhill.

If you let your inhibitions go out the window and allow yourself to go beyond kissing on a first date, you risk canceling out everything you worked for earlier in the evening. Men want what they can't have. So don't just give yourself away. Magnetic women have healthy self-respect and know their value as women.

If you feel like kissing him and he goes in for the lips, then kiss him; but have self-control and know when to press pause, because odds are he won't be the one to stop.

Sweet Good-byes

All of the above having been absorbed in your psyche, you are now ready to learn how to put your personal boundaries into play. So do you kiss or not kiss on a first date? I have done both. I was not in the habit of shaking hands to say good-bye; it felt too cold and businesslike. If I was not romantically interested in my date, I initiated the hug and peck good-bye. If he made my heart beat faster, I'd wait and let him move in for the kiss.

Play by Play

Once you've personally decided what you will allow physically on any first date, you need to know how to handle his advances during the good-bye. First, all dates end in one of two ways: he either walks you to your car or he takes you back home, depending on how your date began. And all date endings involve three moves: *approach, delivery,* and *close.*

If you have decided on a quick, no-kissing conclusion to your evening, then you will need to take the initiative and make the moves to good-bye. While nearing your car or home, find your keys, and get them in position to open your door. As you arrive at your door, put your hand on the door and turn to your man. Offer a polite "thank you" for the date with a sincere compliment about something during the evening. Then smoothly, not harshly or quickly, reach up (*approach*) and kiss him on the cheek, briefly on the lips, or offer a friendly embrace (*delivery*). Release, then look him in the eyes, smile, turn your key and go inside (*close*). Now here is the good part: if you're in your car driving off, wave good-bye. If you're in the lobby of your apartment or condo or you've left him on the curb by your house, turn and wave one more time before you move out of sight (*bonus close*). If he likes you, he'll remain standing there until you disappear. That's a good sign. You've probably accomplished that second date. Approach, delivery, and close.

If you've decided you'll allow him to make the moves and are prepared to put on the brakes when he crosses that invisible line, then you just breathe and let him draw the evening to a close. As he walks you to your door or drops you off at your car, let him open the door, walk you slowly to your destination, and then you can turn to face him and offer your thanks for a good time; then pause and look in his eyes—while you still have your keys ready to open your door (*approach*). Let him take it from there.

Your man will probably say something similar to your thanks and move in for one of the three good-byes I suggested to you, or he'll be nervous and awkward and leave you in the midst of a dramatic pause. An awkward pause is fine, actually very romantic when reminisced. So let a few moments go by if you find yourself in a frozen silence. If he's still just staring at you, thank him again and begin opening your door slowly. If he still has not jumped in with a kiss or embrace, then conclude your evening as planned, with you in control. Offer your kiss on the check or peck on the lips (*delivery*) as you open your door. Turn coyly, smile, and wave good-bye (*close*).

But what if your date slips his hand gently behind your neck and brushes his lips on your forehead, then slides down breathlessly yet surely to meet your lips. Heavy sigh . . . you're in trouble now, because you know you've just been swept off your feet. Whew.

When your man has jumped all over that good-bye and gone in for the heart-stopping embrace, here's a tip on how to handle his advances when he begins to slip past boundaries. Rather than make a scene and act all offended at his nerve, slide your hands over to grab his hands and slightly chuckle as you murmur, "Now, now," or coyly flirt as you say, "I've got to go now; it's been a great evening." And make your smooth but swift exit. Don't linger, or you'll get started all over again. But don't forget to turn and wave one last time as you walk away to see if he is still there with that gleam in his eye.

Practice your good-byes in your mind, even in your bathroom mirror, so you will become smooth and automatic in that approach, delivery, and close. You don't want to be caught off guard or have to think when you are breathlessly swept away. Besides, there's no excuse for losing control because this is a first date. Stay in your right mind, no matter how long it's been since you have felt this way. Be smart, remain focused on your goal for the evening, which is to have him fall head over heals and desire to spend more quality time with you—the inner, real you, not merely your face and body. Don't blow it; rather focus, focus, focus. Stay on task, and don't let the atmosphere sweep you away.

No Sparks: How Do You Let Him Down Easy?

So now you have some guidance on how to handle good-byes with dates with whom you want a second date. The more magnetic you become and the more you practice the secrets I've shared in this book, the more automatic second dates will be. That is flattering, but not always thrilling. So how do you handle dates with guys you don't want to share romantic moments with? Some dates will hold no sparks for you. Has that already happened? Have you enjoyed his company, but there was no physical attraction? I have two remedies for these cases.

My first response is for you to consider giving him another chance. My motto was always, if I couldn't bring myself to kiss the man by date five, I moved on. Until then, if I liked him as a person and enjoyed his company, I kept accepting dates.

If you have absolutely no desire to see him again, there is a polite way to let him know without shattering his ego. Believe it or not, turning snotty or rude usually does *not* work in scaring him away. For some reason, the ones you don't like take bad behavior as a challenge and keep pursuing. (Personally, I think that means they have low self-esteem, but knowing that doesn't help you in your dilemma.)

The classy and kind way to let him down easy and keep both of your egos intact is to begin asking him to describe his ideal mate. Pay close attention to his description, because you may need to clarify what part of that description is obviously not you nor will it ever be. As he describes the mystery woman (even if she sounds conspicuously and deliberately like you), say, "Hmmm, who do I know like that?" and start chatting like buddies setting each other up. You can even say, "If I have a friend matching that description, can I set you two up?"

If he is a classy guy, he will get the picture and say yes or no but remain pleasant the rest of the evening. If he puts you on the spot and wants to know why you don't think you're right together, you don't have a license to be mean. Choose something he mentioned in his ideal-mate description or something true you've heard or observed that isn't personal, such as the two of you have very different goals, faiths, cultures, backgrounds, or interests.

Two of the times I used this approach granted me longtime friends. One such date was so fascinating that we talked for hours and literally stayed until the restaurant closed late that night, yet the romance sparks were not there for me. I could see him with several of my friends, just not me. I began asking about his ideal women and then said, "Hmmm, who do I know that fits that description?" As with my other no-sparks-date-turned-longtime-friend, he went on to marry a beautiful, dynamic lady. The great thing is that since I hadn't kissed either man, it is never awkward around their wives nor was anyone ever really rejected. I just turned the evening around from being a date to being two buddies hanging out. You can let your dates down easy as well, because you are a magnetic classy lady.

Automatic Recap

1. Just because he'll kiss you (or more), does not mean he'll want to see you again.
2. Saying no will transform a womanizer faster than anything else, because no is not something he is used to.
3. Cloud-nine emotions of a kiss do not offer proof of even your own genuine feelings of love for this man.
4. Reflect on your values and boundaries before you leave for your date.
5. Wherever you leave off physically on a first date, sets up the physical progression of the relationship.
6. He'll believe that whatever you do with him on a first date is what you do with all your dates, whether it's true or not.
7. Less is more on a first date, so leave him smiling but wanting more.
8. Skip the insecure people pleasing, and do the uncomfortable—set boundaries. He'll respect you for it and come back for more.
9. Whatever happens physically on a date, the male usually blames the female, since he feels she has more self-control once inhibitions have been lifted.
10. Success in dating is the absence of guilt and the presence of good feelings about yourself and your date.
11. Want to catch the uncatchable? Follow your personal boundaries.
12. Don't believe his "sweet nothing" comments in the heat of passion; it is not his heart speaking.
13. If you will not allow him to kiss you, it's best to initiate the

good-bye gaze, handshake, or peck. If you will allow a kiss, leave the moves to him and be ready to put on the brakes.

14. Let him down easy if there's no sparks. He may be worth another chance.

Etched on His Mind

Can a deep kiss, a tender brush of the lips, a warm embrace, or merely a flirtatious look be enough to etch you on his mind for an automatic second date? Yes it can.

What do you truly want in a date? How do you want to be treated, and what are you looking for? In the very least, magnetic women want second dates, not last minute "come on over" calls. Following my *automatic second date* advice can gain you a second date with just about any man, but more important, with a man worthy of you.

Automatic Journaling
Kiss or Not to Kiss

1. Take a moment to remember your first kiss, and write it in your journal. Write everything you remember about it from who he was, where you were, what you were wearing, how the kiss came about, the details of the kiss itself, and what happened the next time you saw the boy.

2. Reflect on a past date that ended either less than ideally or great but you didn't hear from him again. Write down all you remember about that good-bye. Did you feel like you needed to apologize for anything, or were you guilt free and just disappointed? In hindsight, why do you think that was the end?

3. Describe in detail the ideal first kiss with a man you really like and write *that* in your journal!

4. What are your personal boundaries on any first date? Close your eyes and really think this through. Write down why you drew that particular line. You have to be compelling to convince yourself to stick to the plan when your heart goes aflutter.

5. Visualize how you would *like* your good-bye to go, be it a gaze, peck, kiss, or more. Now revisit my move-by-move descriptions and modify them for what would work for you in each scenario:

   a. You initiate the good-bye with a gaze or peck on the cheek.

   b. You allow him to initiate the embrace, but a dramatic pause occurs for more than a few moments.

   c. You allow him to make the moves, but he starts going too far.

Write each down.

6. Visualize and write out a few ideas for how to let him down easily on that first good-bye if you *don't* want the automatic second date.

10

After the First Date, Just Breathe

Playing It Cool

I n the romantic comedy *50 First Dates* Adam Sandler plays Henry Roth, a veterinarian living in Hawaii who thrives on the company of vacationing women. That is, until he falls for Lucy, played by Drew Barrymore, and leaves his womanizing life behind. The only problem is that Lucy suffers from short-term memory loss and always forgets Henry in the morning. Since she never remembers meeting him, Henry has to do over the first date every single day, hoping one day she'll finally remember him and fall in love for forever. Okay, so maybe the premise is a little unrealistic, but be honest, haven't you at least once wished you could have a do-over of one of your first dates? Maybe even your last first date? You know, practice the evening over and over with that special guy until you get it just right, guaranteeing he'll be calling you back the next day for that automatic second date?

211

The Morning After

Heavy sigh . . . the date went great. You went home, called your girlfriends with every last detail, and updated your journal about your wonderful future with your new man. Now what? When will he call again? And what do you do until then? This chapter covers what to do in the hours, maybe even days, until you hear from him again, as well as what to do when he does or doesn't call.

No matter how much you bonded during your date, you don't really know your guy all that well. You don't know his baggage, you don't know all that is going on in his personal life, and you don't know for sure what he thinks of you thus far. You certainly don't want to scare him away when he's just wading in the shallow end.

Just breathe—and don't you dare call that man. Be sweet if you run into him, but there's no need to call and thank him for the date, even if he spent a lot of money on you. He is the pursuer, not you. No late-night-dialing, girls (you know those impulsive moments you dial his number with just about any silly excuse to chat with your guy)! Call your friends at midnight (if they won't hate you), but don't call that boy. This includes no text messaging. Let him make the next move. It may take a day or even a week for him to feel it's time to call back. What if it's been a week, and your phone hasn't rung? Feels like rejection, ouch! Especially if you're thinking, *But we had the most amazing evening, what could possibly have gone wrong?*

The Detox . . . How Did It Go?

Pull out your journal and write about your date. How did you do in asking questions? What did you learn about him? Was he close to matching your wish list? What things about him are not on your list? You can learn a lot by revisiting and evaluating your date to see what you think you did well, what you think you blew, and what you think you're getting better at. Did you wear your heart on your sleeve, or did you hold back any neediness? Did you slip and reveal that you stalked a past lover or that you desperately want kids by next week or that you have massive credit-card debt you fear you'll never repay? Oops, okay. Try to keep that information to yourself next time, especially on the first two dates!

On the bright side, did you laugh together? Did you flirt and flatter and gaze into his eyes? Did you find out about his childhood, favorite food, or favorite team? Did he tell you a dream or two he has for his future? Did you find out about his values and faith, and did they align with yours? Sometimes we think we had a fabulous time; but when we evaluate the details, we see we have some things to work on in our dating skills. That doesn't mean he won't call back; it just means you know what skills you still need to master. Next time you'll do better.

When He Calls

So he calls back, or maybe even has flowers delivered the next day. Now that is what I'm talking about! This is what you wanted. Congratulations, you have just begun your journey to a potential future with this man.

But hold on. Don't pour all your hopes and dreams into him yet. You are just going for a second date here. Take it slow and don't rush in. You've only been on one date. He is still testing the waters to see if you are someone to invest time in. Don't scare him away. Whatever you do, don't start buying wedding magazines.

What to Say and How to Act

So what do you say on that call? Flattered to hear from him, you will be the same charming girl you were on the date. Don't overdo it and say, "I can't believe you called!" Just continue where you left off. Be warm and friendly. He may or may not ask you for the second date on this follow-up call. It's no big deal if he just calls to say he had a great time and doesn't schedule the next date before he hangs up. He's interested, or he wouldn't have called. He'll call again.

If you miss his call, and he's left a message on your answering machine or voice mail, call back if he asks you to. If he just states, "I had a great time," a response is not necessary other than a smile and a call to your girlfriends to say those two wonderful words—"He called!" And he'll call again. On the other hand, if he sends an e-mail or text message with that message, you can reply, "Me too," or something cute like that.

So many head games are going on in both of you at this stage. You may fear calling back immediately will make you look desperate, and your guy may have buddies telling him, "Hey, man, don't call her for a few days or she'll think you're too anxious and be turned off." Sometimes there's just way too much thinking going on. Let's all relax. The man should call when he feels like calling, be it the next day (which we ladies prefer) or two days later—but come on, within a week, please. And gals, when he calls you, call him back. You're not desperate, you're returning his call.

Don't deliberately miss the call. If you see it's him on caller ID, answer it. But if you do miss it, return the call when it is convenient. You're not required to immediately call back, but it's not a huge deal if you do.

What is the norm for a callback? For me, about 65 percent of the time I'd get called the next day, 25 percent of the time the second day, and 10 percent of the time sometime within a week of the date.

No Last-Minute Dates

Again, no last-minute dates. Just like the first date, you must establish that you are a magnetic, popular woman. You are not available as his last resort or last-minute choice. If he calls at the last minute, chances are someone else turned him down or canceled on him. You are not yet priority number one. The first two dates are the crucial stage of molding his perception of you. If your guy calls on a Thursday or Friday for a weekend date, remember it's best to say you've got plans but would love to see him another time.

He has to think of you first. Let the other women low on his priority list get the last-minute calls; you want to be special. You're not mad; you're just busy. Just because he's had a great time with you on one date doesn't mean he hasn't been seeing someone else. But don't let that threaten you. He doesn't owe you exclusivity at this stage, but as a magnetic woman, you do merit being first choice. He has to figure that out for himself.

By not accepting last-minute get-togethers, you communicate the ever-important message that you are a prize worth winning. In reality, you may just be sitting home rather than seeing him, but this is an important sacrifice for the future of your relationship. You are training him, in an indirect manner, to know that you are worthy of being treated like a lady and not a last-minute hook-up, buddy-buddy, or otherwise. That may mean that you miss out on a date for a week or two until he figures it out. That is perfectly fine and may be necessary in order for him to learn to call in plenty of time. It will pay off in the long run.

Ugh, When Can I Call Him?

Okay, okay, so you are using every ounce of self-control to keep from picking up that phone or sending that text message or e-mail. When can you contact him? Right after his first move following your first date, you are free to follow up.

That first move may be a phone call, text message, or e-mail. Or he may stop by your place of work. The very best follow-up to your first date is for him to send you a thank-you gift in the way of flowers, candy, or unique gift relevant to something you discussed on your date. If a man has really enjoyed your company, it is not uncommon for him to show his appreciation by having something delivered to you. It is not required and doesn't mean he doesn't like you if a gift is not sent. It just means you really made an impression, and he is a real classy guy if he does send a gift.

Notice that I said *he* sends *you* the thank-you gift—not the reverse! Sure, the guy paid for the first date. That is the way things are. But that doesn't mean you follow up with a thank-you call or gift. You allow the man to keep on with the pursuit. You want him to be grateful that he got to spend time with you— because *you* are a magnetic woman!

While I always beamed when roses were delivered (a dozen roses can keep you on cloud nine all week, no matter how stressful your work environment), my absolutely most charming after-the-first-date gift came at a time when my roommate and I were being stalked by a rapist. Obviously, that information came out during our date. I also shared that although I'm a major do-it-yourselfer who proudly owns her own drill, I hadn't had a chance to put a peep hole in my apartment door. When our receptionist buzzed in to say I had a delivery the next day, my assistant and I were absolutely charmed at the thought that went into his gift. He sent me a copper peep hole, complete with the appropriate drill bit. Included was a note saying to call him to set up a time for him to install it for me. That was good, wasn't it?

If your office or home is graced with a special delivery the day after your first date, woo hoo! Way to go, girl! I hope you are beaming. This is indeed as much a first move as a phone call. You can and *should* respond by calling or texting to offer your thanks (e-mail is too slow a response).

What If He Doesn't Call?

My friend Samantha is a five foot eight, beautiful blonde who rarely has a problem attracting a first date. It's the second that is hard to come by. Needlessly insecure, she insists on calling the day after every first date, whether she likes the guy or not. She can't let it go. Believe me, I have done everything I can to prevent her from making that call, but she just can't help her compulsion. Then she continues pursuing until he stops taking her calls. Yet she is surprised that she's still single ten years later. It's not because she's not a great gal. The problem is that she never allows a man to miss or pursue her. I fear she will remain single forever unless she changes.

You've evaluated the first date and are convinced it went great. Your head was spinning when you got home, and you slept with a smile swept across your face after you called your girlfriends to relive every detail of the evening. He may have even said, "I had a great time; I'll call you," as he kissed you goodnight.

But it's two days later—no, a week later—and your phone still has not rung *nor* have flowers been delivered on your doorstep. Rejection—ouch! Now what? What is going on, and what can you do to fix it?

Don't You Dare Call Him

Just breathe. And don't you dare call that man. You may be saying, "But we had the most amazing evening. What could possibly have gone wrong?" Relax and read on.

Remember the *Friends* episode[1] when Chandler was set up with Rachel's boss? Chandler didn't exactly enjoy his date, yet he didn't know how to end it. Not only was Chandler a clumsy, nice guy but the date was a setup by his close friend, so he couldn't be rude and upset Rachel. The scene offered great comedic timing as Chandler did everything he could to just kiss her on the cheek and say goodnight. But she just stood there at his door staring at him. Finally he said, "Okay, I'll call you." When he didn't call, Rachel's boss was perplexed and kept pressuring Rachel about what went wrong. The show concluded with his taking her on another date after he'd promised Rachel he would end it without uttering those two lying words, "I'll call." But when the date ended, same scenario, same good-bye. Some guys don't know how else to end a date other than saying that generic, "I'll call," knowing it is as meaningless to them as their daily greeting of, "How are you?"

Dr. Patricia Allen has great insight into why some men don't call back, even when they give all the blatant signs that they will. She claims that a man's body is on that date, but his soul often is not, which means his mind is elsewhere. Most men, she says, have a hard time thinking and feeling at the same time. So "on the first few dates he's not likely to be thinking about you as a whole person. Rather what he's mostly feeling is lust. . . . Later when he's alone . . . , he can begin to think about you as a human being. It is then that he may decide that, for whatever reason, you and he are not right for each other."[2]

Reevaluate His Body Language

Since he hasn't called back, it may be time to reevaluate the first date. Think about how his body language supported or contradicted his words. Communication expert Dr. Lillian Glass says, "The body tells you a great deal about yourself and others. Gestures, posture, and body position mean something because these signals are the body's attempt to bring suppressed feelings to the surface . . . whether you know it or not. Body language can reinforce or contradict verbal messages because a person's body discloses true feelings."[3]

So, ladies, when your date's body language contradicts his words, you should believe the body language. Body language reveals how we really feel, while our words are sometimes calculated and concealing. Did he offer you insincere clichés such as a welcoming, "How are you" or "I'll call you"? If so, did his body language confirm or dismiss his sincerity? Think about it, and be honest with what you truly observed rather than what you hoped he meant.

No Explanation Needed

Yes, I know. When he doesn't call back, you want to know what went wrong, and you feel you just have to get an explanation. No, you don't. If he didn't call you back because of something you did to scare him away, he's not going to tell you. And if he says it's because he's got too much in his life right now to get involved, that may or may not be true. It's hard for most people to tell you hurtful things. Unless he is Simon Cowell, he's not going to want to tell you hurtful things. It's best just to be nice and move on, until or unless you hear from him again.

Desperate Housewives star Teri Hatcher handled such a scenario in a very smart and sophisticated manner that you will do well to adopt. After the paparazzi had captured a photograph of her and *American Idol*'s Ryan Seacrest kissing in Malibu, Seacrest's later rejection of her was splashed across the headlines of all the tabloids, making her humiliation seem tougher than the average gal's. The twosome had gone out three times. Seacrest didn't ask her out a fourth time. She took the high road and maintained a great attitude—at least publicly. Three cheers for a classy lady! When confronted on national TV about how she felt about not getting called back, she told Dayna Devon on *Extra* TV that early on in a relationship there is no obligation. "No one should have to explain. You go on the very beginning one, two, three dates with somebody, and nobody has to explain why they don't want to go on date four. And he didn't want to go on date four,"[4] said Hatcher.

So she kissed him. Wouldn't you? Take relationships slow. You are *not* exclusive until you both verbally agree that you are. Unless or until such time as you verbally agree to date only each other, you are both free to date others or simply move on without ripping the other's heart out. So guard your heart, take it slow, and definitely maintain enough self-control to not do anything you would regret if the relationship ends tomorrow.

Let It Go

If time has passed and your guy still has not called you for a second date, you have to let it go. No matter how much it still bugs you, don't call him and ask for an explanation. Don't tell him off when you run into him in public. Just remain your same magnetic self. It will pay off in the future, perhaps the very near future.

He may be in the midst of some heavy personal stuff or pre-occupied with his career. He could be in the midst of a breakup, another new courtship, a major work deadline, or a messy family situation. He may also just be a creep who is unworthy of you and is doing you a major favor by bowing out early. Or it just may not be the best timing for you two. After one date, you cannot fully know what is really going on in his life. Accept that and be cool.

Whatever his reason, give him his space and time to miss you. If he truly had a great time with you, he'll remember and will call when he can give you quality time. And if you've established that he needs to book you early in the week, then he already *knows* not to call at the last minute, because you are a happening gal and have things going on. This is a good thing.

When your date doesn't call right back, just breathe and move on. He could call anytime, in a few weeks, in six months, or not at all. Go on with your life, pursue other dates, and let it go. The way you handle what appears to be rejection may be just the thing that gets your guy in the end! Hang in there. Be positive, and refuse to let bitterness or insecurity take over.

When Your Paths Cross

Next time you see him, make sure you are as polite and magnetic as you were on that first date. Even if it's six months later, be charming and don't ask what happened. If you see him someplace across the room, smile and say hi, but don't go out of your way to pursue the conversation. Make eye contact, flirt, and compel him to come to you.

If this date was to be the love of your life, you will get another chance with him. It was only one date. Next time your paths cross, be pleasant, not overly excited, not angry, but pleasant.

222 CHAPTER 10: AFTER THE FIRST DATE, JUST BREATHE

And don't play games as though you don't recognize him—that is the ultimate giveaway of insecurity. Simply say hi and ask how he is doing.

If He *Never* Calls Back

Sometimes, no matter what you do, a date has no intention of seeing you again. The chemistry is just not there. Of the three men who didn't ask me out for the second date during my eighteen months of countless blind dates, one was a cute creep who clearly did not like me, nor I him. But there was a chemistry between us that kept us wasting our time long enough to complete the evening and even kiss. Can you believe it? I kissed him because he was cute—cute like *Grey's Anatomy's* McDreamy—even though neither of us liked each other. Shall we say, *dumb*?

Another of the blind dates who didn't call me back was a successful, extremely talented, funny guy who shared my faith. He wasn't my type nor I his, but I was still attracted to him and enjoyed my date. I definitely would have gone out with him again if he would have pursued it. Though we clearly had different backgrounds and life plans, my ego was still quite bruised when he didn't call for that second date. I guess he was more mature and knew there was no romance there for him. We ran into each other several times after that, and because I maintained my cool, we became friends. He even did some favors for me (performed at a charity event for free and offered autographs for friends— very cool). I have absolutely nothing bad to say about him. He just didn't like me in "that way." It happens.

Don't feel bad if you blow it a time or two. Think of how

many times a home-run champion struck out before he even got a hit. You are practicing your magnetic-woman skills. You will get better the more you date.

Don't Scold Him for Blowing You Off

I mentioned in the introduction that I had few dates until after college. Perhaps one of the reasons was because I hadn't yet learned how to get that second date. When I was eighteen, I had a first date with that thirty-one-year-old Grammy-winning gospel singer I mentioned in chapter 5. He said wonderful things to me, including that I was beautiful, had long pretty fingers, etc. etc. I ate it up. He even kissed me rather romantically. Wow, I was smitten. I went home dreaming of my life on the road with my singer. The date couldn't have gone better. I was sure he was in love.

He didn't call back. I was devastated.

I knew where he went to church when he was not on the road, so I showed up there about three months later. I am embarrassed to say that I went up to him in the lobby and told him off for saying all those sweet things, kissing me, and then dumping me. "You shouldn't say those things to an impressionable girl if you don't mean them," I scolded. Yes, I confess, I actually did that.

Don't make the same mistake. You're better than that. I was naive and immature. I didn't have this book. But you do. Even though I am still the same person I was back then, my interpersonal skills have improved. This is what I yearn for you. Accept that something can go wrong at any of the three stages of a first date—before, during, or after. If it does, know that it's not because you are lacking as a person. You two are just not meant to be together, and you got to find out a little early. Don't let one missed connection mess up your life. If and when a first date does not call you for a second, relax. Don't call him. Be sweet if you see him, use self-control to prevent the "late night dialings," keep from getting bitter, and begin looking for your next first date.

If you get bitter, track him down, and tell him off, you blow any chance with him and mess up your attitude about men in general. Inevitably those emotions will spill over to your next date. Remember attitude is important! A great attitude will pay off soon enough, either with this man calling you back or a new guy sweeping you off your feet. And you want to be in a positive frame of mind when he does.

If you keep your cool and stay nice, you keep the door open for your man to change his mind about not calling and to step up and pursue you in the near future.

Give Yourself a Break

Ladies, we tend to overanalyze everything. Don't be too hard on yourself. I love Dr. Laura Schlessinger's perspective on how some ladies handle relationships. "Far too many women behave more like beggars than choosers in the dating game. For them, dating is a process of hoping-to-be-selected rather than an opportunity to select."[5]

Dr. Schlessinger is right. See yourself as the one doing the selecting, rather than waiting your whole life to be selected. When you make your man the focus of the first and second date, it is for your own purposes: you are trying to ascertain whether he is good enough for you. There's no need to walk on eggshells around him or con him into thinking you are worthy of him. You *are* worthy of him. The skills I've taught in the past nine chapters not only allow him to see your amazing magnetic qualities, but they allow you to get close enough to him to see if *he* is as magnetic on the inside as he appears on the outside. So if you are rejected by your date, chalk it up to his not being the one you are looking for.

Refuse to allow rejection to define you—because it doesn't. It is an *occurrence*, not a *definition*. Rejection doesn't mean we are not worthy of a man. It just means that you and that particular man are not right for each other. There is someone better out there for you. If you made mistakes on the date, learn from them, and try not to repeat them on your next first date. There will be others. Go back to the Male GPS chapter and get back to flirting. Your automatic second date awaits you.

Automatic Recap

1. After the first date, relax, lean on your friends, and don't you dare call your man.
2. Reminisce on your date and grade yourself on how you did on your dating skills.
3. Although a man wants to know you like him, he doesn't want you pursuing him. That's his job. Just relax.
4. If you run into him before he's called you back, act casual and pleasant, with no bad vibes.
5. Don't panic if he takes a few days or even a week to call back. Guys have their own head trips playing out while dating.
6. When he calls, take it slow. Be happy to hear from him, but remember to pace yourself. You're just moving on to a second date, not a wedding.

7. Remember—no last-minute dates, not even for a second date.

8. If he sends you flowers or a thank-you gift, be classy and call or text message with your thanks.

9. Another reason to play it cool after a long silence following a first date is that he may just be tying up loose ends in his life and intend to call back when that occurs. Keep dating others and see how you feel if and when he reappears.

10. Don't scold him if you think he's blown you off. Take the high road and let it go.

11. If he doesn't call back, feel the pain and consider that date as a training session. Refuse bitterness and move on. You're a magnetic woman, so turn on your Male GPS and say, "Next!"

On Your Way

After the date is over, go home, write about it in your journal, call your girlfriends, and keep living your life. If you've followed my secrets, you can expect to hear from your man before you can blink. If you don't, you will survive. You've narrowed your field and come one date closer to Mr. Right.

Automatic Journaling
After-the-First-Date Journaling

1. Time to detox from your last date. Pull out your journal and write all about your date. How did it go and how did you do with these new skills you're working on? What things about him are not on your list? What do you think you blew, where are you improving, and what did you do extremely well? Grade yourself.

2. Based on his words during the date, when do you expect him to call you back? When would you be disappointed if you still haven't heard? If he said "I'll call," what was his body language when he said those words?

3. While the first date is fresh in your mind, quickly write any clues he gave you that something may be going on in his life right now to keep him from jumping headfirst into a relationship: Is work crazy right now? Is he a single dad? Is he just ending a relationship? Is there a family crisis? Any other clues? Revisit this if a week or more goes by without a call.

4. Reminisce and write about three of your previous first dates who called you back. How long was it before you heard from each? Did he send a thank-you gift? Did you call before he had a chance? Did you thank him before he had a chance to thank you? How did that turn out for you?

5. Think through how you will respond when your next first date calls you back. How will you greet him? What if it is one week later or even one month? What will you do and say to prevent a snippy attitude or overexuberance from hearing his voice on the line?

6. List three people you can call next time you really have the

urge to call your new guy. Put their names and numbers on a Post-it and stick it to the phones you use most often (even if you know their numbers by heart—it's there to remind you in your moment of weakness).

7. If this guy or the last guy didn't call back, write down specifically how that made you feel. Now write what about him was not ideal for you. There's got to be something about him that was not on your list. He probably did you a favor. Feel the pain, improve on what you need to improve on for the next date, and refuse bitterness by being thankful you learned a lesson without blowing it with the man of your dreams! (If he was the man of your dreams, he'd still be around.)

Epilogue

After the Second Date

Keep Him Pursuing You

n *How to Lose a Guy in 10 Days,* Kate Hudson's character, Andie Anderson, covers the "How To" beat for *Composure* magazine and is assigned to write an article on "How to lose a guy in 10 days." The inspiration for the article is Andie's best friend, Michelle, also a reporter at *Composure.* Apparently, Michelle doesn't have a problem getting first dates; she has a problem getting second, third, and fourth dates. As soon as her guy calls back for that second date, she is convinced of his love and becomes obsessive, clingy, whiny, nagging, critical . . . you get the picture. Unfortunately, Michelle is not just a fictional character. Many women blow it at love with the same actions. But you don't have to be one of the statistics.

❊

Just because you've gotten that sought-after second date doesn't mean you've locked up that adorable man's heart. Hold off on "I love you," skip the subscription to *Bride* magazine, refrain from hanging his picture on your wall, and don't try to mold him into what you want him to be. Play it cool, get to know him, and keep accepting other first dates.

Your man is just testing the waters. Even if you are his current obsession, you cannot believe his hype. Force your new romance to go slow, or it will definitely fizzle out before the next change of season.

How should you act beyond the second date? When is it safe to let your guard down and spill your guts about your feelings, your hopes, your baggage, and your past? Think of your developing relationship as running a marathon—and pace yourself. If you sprint from the gate, neither of you will make it to the finish line. Take it slow but sure.

Continue practicing these dating skills. Keep pursuing your life goals. Keep becoming more and more magnetic. And keep your life going outside of your new relationship. On each successive date, reveal a little bit more about yourself and give another piece of your heart—but just one piece at a time.

As time goes by, when you've shared laughter and tears, a few ups and downs, and developed a basis of trust and friendship, you can let your guard down more. By the third or fourth date, you should be sharing as much about your life as he is about his. You can also feel free to cook him a meal, pick up a tab, or do something nice for him, as long as you don't overdo it. A nice rule of thumb is to reciprocate about every third or fourth date. That way he never feels he owes you. He remains the pursuer and you the pursued.

Remember that boys always want what they can't have. They need a challenge. Stay a little bit out of reach. Encourage him, but don't drown him. Don't just *play* hard to get, *be* hard to get because you keep living and still maintain an active life outside of your new love.

And don't dial his number. Until you've been on more than a dozen dates, don't initiate phone calls. After you've been dating awhile, you can call him every once in a while, but still leave it to him to set the pace. Until a man has given you his heart, he is not fully yours. Until that happens, you want him actively pursuing you. You are not in an exclusive relationship until you both have mutually agreed upon it. If you are getting too emotionally involved and fear he is not as involved, keep yourself as busy as you can with friends, social activities, and even more first dates. If you keep busy while you're getting to know your new man, you won't come across as desperate; hence, you won't scare him away. Until you're in an established relationship, don't accept any last-minute dates. You still want to project that mystery and that hard-to-get vibe so you'll remain a challenge. You are a woman who knows what she wants and insists on being treated like the magnetic woman she is.

If you slip and initiate a call or e-mail, don't call or e-mail again until you've heard from him. Keep paying attention to your guy and what he reveals about himself. You want to know the truth of what you're getting. Anyone can play a role for about six weeks—after that, the real person emerges. So if he suddenly turns into someone else, don't assume it's something you've done. Your man may have just relaxed enough to let the real person shine through. Pay attention, enjoy the ride, and keep working on your dating skills.

Dr. Phil is so right when he says, "A guy doesn't value a woman if he doesn't have anything invested in her. That is why guys suddenly want a woman that they didn't even notice as soon as someone else shows interest in her."[1]

Besides, the longer you keep your own heart at bay, the longer you can remain objective and see if this guy really is *all that* on the inside. It takes time to know if he's worth keeping or deserves ditching! I stand firm on the advice I gave in *Finding a Man Worth Keeping*. There I advised you not to see your new guy more than two or three times a week during the first few months of active dating. Pick up a copy of that book for more detailed guidance on how to move your new love from date two on down the aisle of matrimony.

Keep going on first dates until you find your man-worth-keeping and he gives you his heart. The more you date, the more you'll be able to fine-tune your ideal-man wish list.

You are beginning a covert race of chasing your man until he catches you! So fasten your seatbelt and get ready for the ride of your life! If you master these skills, your man may never know you saw him first. At the very least, you will see your repeat-date ratio skyrocket. Enjoy the ride, and keep your eyes open.

Keep on growing, keep on dating, and before long you'll progress from your automatic second date into the arms of the man of your dreams.

Now, step out and show the world of eligible bachelors your newly discovered magnetic self. And remember to cut yourself some slack. Dating is supposed to be fun. You are striving to arrive at your true fabulous self, while looking for the one deserving of you.

Send me your stories at www.automaticdate.com. I'd love to hear about your journeys to automatic second dates.

Addendum

Discovering Who You Are
Finding Your True Worth

iden·ti·ty
The set of qualities that make a person different
from other people. Children begin to form their own
identity by the age of two.[1]

Has life handed you a raw deal? Has your self-worth been beat down from the day you were born? If you struggle with your identity and especially your self-worth, this addendum is for you. I have written these pages to help you turn the tide, say enough is enough, and take the reigns of your identity. If the pages of this book have not yet compelled you to rise above your adversity, these next pages will.

So, I ask, who are you? In whom or what have you placed your identity? How did you form your image? Perhaps you bought into the illusions of fashion magazines and celebrity tabloids that promised you could be happy if you just look like that or wear this brand of heels or carry that style of purse. Maybe you've spent your life trying to measure up to someone else's expectations, and when you fall short, you allow his or her opinion to demolish your self-worth. Or maybe you feel as if something is missing in your life—as though there is a hole inside you that needs to be filled, and you are unable to fill it.

You Matter!

First and foremost, I want you to know that *you* matter! You are one of a kind. No other human being is exactly like you. No one has your same DNA. You are truly unique and have something to offer the world (and that includes men). And until you get that and learn to love *yourself* and what you have to offer, you will not attract dates worthy of the magnetic woman who's been hiding inside you!

After all you've been through and after all the pain you've suffered, isn't it time you discover the good life? If you just hesitated, let me answer for you—yes! Absolutely yes!

You will never become what you're not willing to pursue. It takes conscious effort. It goes back to attitude and courage, girl. You have but one life to live, so starting this very moment you are going to live it to the fullest. No man, past hurts, present challenges, or potential rejection is going to stop you now. From this moment on, choose to face your fear, no matter how scary and uncomfortable, and become the magnetic person you have hidden inside, as you courageously read on.

A huge step toward discovering your dynamic, magnetic self lies in looking back at the road that got you here. You can't get where you want to go until you know where you've been! So I offer you a guide for exploring your life thus far, as you pursue the life you always dreamed of.

It's Your Life! Write about It!

Pull out your journal or a fresh notebook and begin writing your autobiography. You don't have to be a dynamic writer for this exercise. Just move your pencil on the page or your fingers on the keyboard and reminisce on your life thus far. You will find a guide at the end of this addendum to copy and paste into your journal to help you as you write your life story.

You will be amazed at what is revealed as you write. Things you didn't remember and insights you hadn't yet comprehended will come to you as you experience many "aha" moments.

It may take you one day, one month, or more, but I urge you to get up every morning and carve out time to work through your autobiography. It will reveal hidden patterns and past pain that have been subconsciously driving you where you didn't want to go. By taking an honest look at what has been, you can make a conscious choice regarding what will be. And more important, you will discover what or who is missing!

Created and Loved

If you haven't figured it out by now, I'm one of those who believes in a literal, personal, living God who created the universe. And not only did He create this vast universe and everything in it, He also created you and me. You are no accident, regardless of the love or lack thereof you received from your parents.

One of my most cherished scriptures is Psalm 139, right smack in the middle of the Bible. As you read this excerpt, written by King David several thousand years ago, I want you to know that these words are true about you, personally, today!

*O LORD, you have searched me
and you know me.*

*You know when I sit and when I rise;
you perceive my thoughts from afar.*

*You discern my going out and my lying down;
you are familiar with all my ways.*

*Before a word is on my tongue
you know it completely, O LORD. . . .*

*Where can I go from your Spirit?
Where can I flee from your presence?*

*If I go up to the heavens, you are there;
if I make my bed in the depths, you are there.*

*If I rise on the wings of the dawn,
if I settle on the far side of the sea,*

*even there your hand will guide me,
your right hand will hold me fast.*

*If I say, "Surely the darkness will hide me
and the light become night around me,"*

*even the darkness will not be dark to you;
the night will shine like the day,
for darkness is as light to you.*

*For you created my inmost being;
you knit me together in my mother's womb.*

*I praise you because I am fearfully and
wonderfully made. . . .*

My frame was not hidden from you
when I was made in the secret place. . . .

Your eyes saw my unformed body.
All the days ordained for me
were written in your book
before one of them came to be.[2]

God Cares about Your Pain

Let's face it, life is hard—for some more than others! But let me tell you this: just as bad things do happen to good people, there is a God who sees and cares and who has a personal plan for your life—and He wants you to know Him personally. I'm not talking about religion; I'm talking about a relationship.

I've had my own share of drama in my life, including devastating heartbreaks, financial crises, a severe burn, recurring medical scares, malicious verbal attacks, being stalked by a rapist, the loss of dreams, loss of friendships, and more. A verse that has gotten me through difficult times such as these is:

Be anxious for nothing, but in everything by prayer
and supplication, with thanksgiving, let your
requests be made known to God; and the peace of
God, which surpasses all understanding, will guard
your hearts and minds through Christ Jesus.[3]

After mastering the dating skills to achieve automatic second dates, dating became a glorious, exciting, busy pastime for me.

Yet, to be frank, at times it left me feeling shallow and unfulfilled, because even though there was a *quantity* of men in my life, the *quality* of character in the men I was dating was lacking. Though I'd spent time with a Grammy-winning rock star, an Academy Award–winning actor, a top music promoter, and a professional golfer, my life was empty. By the end of my twenties, no one in my life fit my list for "Mr. Right." You see, I had made a special promise at a very young age.

A Life-Changing Prayer

It was a Sunday evening. I was seven years old, and the pastor of the church where I grew up made a profound statement. He said, "There comes a time in the life of every person when you have to stop just following the religion of your parents and make a decision for yourself. What are you going to do about Jesus? You have a choice. You can either accept Him or reject Him, but you will decide."

At that very moment, even at my young age, I knew it was my time to make the choice to believe Jesus was real and invite Him into my life. I said a simple prayer:

Dear Jesus, I need you. I've messed up and done things that Mommy and Daddy don't know about, and I want You to forgive me. I want You to be my God, not just the God of my parents. I believe You died on the cross for me and came back to life three days later and still live today. Please take over my life and help me be who You want me to be. In Jesus's name, amen.

That prayer was so simple, and yet it changed my life forever. And Jesus has been my closest friend ever since. Throughout each tragedy of my life, God has given me a peace that passes all understanding. Jesus is my true security in an insecure, scary world. Though others have left me, He never will.

A Future and a Hope

In my twenties I would never have dared dream I'd get to experience the life I'm living now. No, I'm not talking about the traveling or writing books or meeting all the neat people I get to meet; I'm talking about this amazing husband and two children I've been blessed with. God has been good to me.

It is always darkest before the dawn. When you're at the bottom, the only way to look is up. Keep that on the forefront of your mind during your storms, and look up to God.

I don't know what storm you may be in the middle of right now, but I can guarantee you one thing: though *we* don't know the future, God does! An ancient proverb tells us that we can keep making our plans but none of us knows how they will turn out.[4] Only God knows. He knows the future.

The Jewish prophet Jeremiah proclaimed that God has a plan for each of us, plans for good and not for evil, plans for a future and a hope.[5] We have to be willing and have the courage to keep moving forward, no matter what happens. Refuse to settle, and never give up! You must persevere to achieve the life you dream of.

That is how I have lived my life. A hectic career is not easy. Bad things do happen to good people. But I've learned many valuable lessons in my life. I've learned that Jesus loves me even when I'm ugly and no one else seems to care. I've learned that Jesus loves me when I fail Him and let Him down. Most important of all, I learned that even when I'm rejected by this date or that date or this friend or that family member, Jesus is faithful. He said, "Never will I leave you; never will I forsake you."[6] My career, in fact my entire life, has been about perseverance and God's faithfulness to me.

We all face hardships in life. The difference is that some of us have had the privilege of having a personal encounter with God. Not only have I discovered this, but many of my family members, friends, colleagues, and acquaintances who have been through far worse experiences than I, have also discovered this secret. You can read some of their true stories in my book *The Day I Met God* (available at www.victoryarogers.com, www .amazon.com, and www.randomhouse.com). Like me, these people have found purpose, strength, and peace in the midst of devastating circumstances. I want that peace for you too.

God did not create us as robots with no will of our own, and He won't force you or anyone to believe in Him. God allows us each to make our own decisions about all areas of our lives. But our choices have consequences—and making choices means experiencing those consequences, as well as the consequences of the actions of those around us. A simple reflection on history or observation of our society today reveals that there is, indeed, evil in this world. I also believe there is a literal devil and that he and his invisible legion of demons are trying to destroy us, just as the Bible proclaims.

St. John tells us in the New Testament that "The thief comes only to steal and kill and destroy; I [Jesus] have come that they [YOU] may have life, and have it to the full."[7] Isn't it time you stop allowing evil to win over your life and turn your life over to the One who wants you to live a fulfilling and abundant life right here and now? The following excerpt from the apostle Paul's letter to the Romans gives us the solution we need, as we face our own identity crisis:

> *Anyone, of course, who has not welcomed this invisible but clearly present God, the Spirit of Christ, won't know what we're talking about. But for you who welcome him, in whom he dwells—even though you still experience all the limitations of sin—you yourself experience life on God's terms. It stands to reason, doesn't it, that if the alive-and-present God who raised Jesus from the dead moves into your life, he'll do the same thing in you that he did in Jesus, bringing you alive to himself? . . . That's why I don't think there's any comparison between the present hard times and the coming good times. . . .*
>
> *If we don't know how or what to pray, it doesn't matter. [The Spirit of God] does our praying in and for us, making prayer out of our wordless sighs, our aching groans. He knows us far better than we know ourselves . . . and keeps us present before God. That's why we can be so sure that every detail in our lives of love for God is worked into something good. . . .*
>
> *So, what do you think? With God on our side like this, how can we lose? . . . I'm absolutely convinced that nothing—nothing living or dead, angelic or demonic, today or tomorrow, high or low, thinkable or unthinkable—absolutely nothing can get between us and God's love.*[8]

Invite Him In

You, too, can experience a life of true inner peace and happiness despite your present or past circumstances. It's available simply for the asking. Jesus makes an announcement in the book of Revelation, the last book of the Bible: "Here I am! I stand at the door and knock. If anyone hears my voice and opens the door, I will come in."[9] Won't you do that right now? Invite him in by repeating a prayer like the prayer I prayed as a young girl.

"Dear Jesus, I need You. I've messed up and done things that no one else knows about except You. Please forgive me. I want You to be my God, not just the God of my parents. I believe You died on the cross for me and came back to life three days later and still live today. Please take over my life and help me be who You want me to be. In Jesus's name, amen."

A New Life

Congratulations on having the courage to begin a new and exciting adventure in your life. Your life will never be the same! You have a new identity that reveals your incredible worth. Continue pursuing your relationship with God by talking to Him daily (that's what I call prayer) and reading His life manual, the Bible (begin with the New Testament, which is about three-fourths of the way through the book; then read the Old Testament).

I truly believe you did not read this book, and especially this addendum, by accident. May the writing of your autobiography allow you to further understand your worth to God and lead you to a deeper relationship with God who created you, as you continue your journey to the person you were meant to be.

Enjoy your new venture in discovering life as a confident, magnetic woman. Dating, not to mention getting automatic second dates, will take on a whole new meaning for you—and that is exactly what you want!

The Journey to Who You Are

It's easier to recall your past when you look back on small age spans. You can choose to go in chronological order or skip around, as long as you eventually answer all the questions for each age span. To get started on your autobiography, begin with any age span listed below and answer each question to the best of your ability: ages 0–5; grades 1–4; grades 5 and 6; junior high school; high school; ages 18–21/college years; your 20s, 30s, 40s, 50s, 60s, and beyond.

Some Guidelines
Don't edit yourself as you go. Don't overthink. Just start writing the first thing that comes to mind when you think back to that age and ask yourself each question listed. When you are finished, you're ready to put it all into chronological order and write the story of your life, with all the new insights and lessons you've discovered in this journey to your identity and self-worth.

Some very painful memories may come up. Don't be surprised if the hurt feelings come back while you're writing. Just feel the pain and keep going. It's important to recall and write down how you made it through those times and what you learned along the way, so you can understand how you became who you are today.

Your Questions

1. What do you remember most, good or bad, about your life through this age span?
2. What did you do?
3. Where did you live?
4. Who were your friends and enemies?
5. What highs did you experience?
6. What lows did you experience?
7. How did you view God, and what role did you see God playing in your life at that time?
8. What were some of your life's blessings, joys, and victories?
9. What were your biggest disappointments, hurts, and storms?
10. What dreams were planted in your heart?
11. Did you pursue those dreams? If not, who or what stopped you?
12. If you met God during this age span, when did you meet Him, and what led up to your inviting Him into your life?

May you enjoy your journey to the real you!

Further Reading

The Day I Met God by Jim Covell, Karen Covell, and Victorya Michaels Rogers

The Dream Giver by Bruce Wilkinson

Everything You Always Wanted to Know About God by Eric Metaxas

How to Win Friends and Influence People by Dale Carnegie

People of the Lie by M. Scott Peck

The Purpose Driven Life by Rick Warren

The Road Less Traveled by M. Scott Peck

Seizing Your Divine Moment by Erwin Raphael McManus
The Treasure Principle by Randy Alcorn
When We Hurt by Philip Yancey

Helpful Web sites:
www.mantokeep.com
www.needhim.org
www.familylife.com
www.family.org

Notes

Introduction

1. www.merriam-webster.com.
2. 1 Corinthians 9:24–25 (MSG).

Chapter 1: The Magnetic Woman

1. www.merriam-webster.com.
2. Proverbs 23:7 (NKJV).
3. http://thinkexist.com/quotes/charles_f._swindoll/.
4. www.merriam-webster.com.
5. Ibid.
6. Dr. Phil McGraw, *Love Smart: Find the One You Want—Fix the One You Got* (New York: Free Press, 2005), 10.
7. www.visualthesaurus.com; and www.merriam-webster.com.
8. www.merriam-webster.com.
9. Ibid.

Chapter 2: The Eye of the Beholder

1. www.merriam-webster.com.
2. Nancy Etcoff, *Survival of the Prettiest: The Science of Beauty* (New York: First Anchor Books, July 2000).
3. www.etonline.com/celebrities/spotlight/37719/indes.html.

4. Ibid.
5. Ibid.
6. *First for Women*, "How I Came Out on Top Even Though Everyone Said I Was Too Fat," April 16, 2007, 41.
7. Ibid., 40.
8. Ecclesiastes 3:1.
9. www.etonline.com/fashion/news/38103/.

Chapter 4: A Little Help from My Friends
1. 1 Peter 5:8.

Chapter 6: On Your Mark, Get Set . . .
1. Luke 6:31.
2. John Gray, *Men Are from Mars, Women Are from Venus* (New York: HarperCollins, 1992), 53.

Chapter 7: You Had Me at Hello
1. James 1:19.
2. Barbara Walters, *How to Talk with Practically Anybody about Practically Anything* (Garden City, NY: Doubleday, 1970), 191–82.

Chapter 8: Let the Sparks Fly!
1. Dr. Phil McGraw, *Love Smart: Find the One You Want—Fix the One You Got* (New York: Free Press, 2005), 179–80.
2. Tracy Cabot, *How to Make a Man Fall in Love with You* (New York: Dell, 1984), 152.
3. Eleanore Case, "Love Special: Six Ways to Woo Your Lover," *New Scientist*, April 27, 2006, 46.

Chapter 9: To Kiss or Not to Kiss

1. John Gray, *Mars and Venus on a Date* (New York Harper-Collins, 1997), 165.
2. Ibid., 181.
3. Ibid., 159–60.
4. Ibid.
5. Josh McDowell and Paul Lewis, *Givers, Takers and other Kinds of Lovers* (Wheaton, IL: Living Books, 1982), 88.
6. Genesis 3:12.

Chapter 10: After the First Date, Just Breathe

1. *Friends* episode #3.20, "The One with the Dollhouse," originally aired 4/10/97.
2. Dr. Patricia Allen and Sandra Harmon, *Getting to "I Do": The Secret to Doing Relationships Right!* (New York: Avon Books, 1994), 115–16.
3. Lillian Glass, PhD, *I Know What You're Thinking: Using the Four Codes of Reading People to Improve Your Life* (New York: John Wiley, 2002), 147.
4. *Extra* TV, Warner Brothers, May 3, 2006, interview with *Extra*'s Dayna Devon, http://telepixtvcgi.warnerbros.com/v2/news/0506/03/1/text.html.
5. Dr. Laura Schlessinger, *10 Stupid Things Women Do to Mess Up Their Lives* (New York: Villard, 1994), 29.

Epilogue

1. Dr. Phil McGraw, *Love Smart: Find the One You Want—Fix the One You Got* (New York: Free Press, 2005), 185.

Addendum

1. www.dictionary.com.
2. Psalm 139:1–16 (FYI: When you see a number followed by a

colon, it means "chapter number: verse number" of the book referenced).

3. Philippians 4:6–7 (NKJV).
4. Proverbs 16:9.
5. Jeremiah 29:11.
6. Hebrews 13:5.
7. John 10:10.
8. Romans 8:9–38 (MSG).
9. Revelation 3:20.

About the Author

Dating and relating coach Victorya Michaels Rogers is also the author of *Finding a Man Worth Keeping*. She spent more than a decade as a Hollywood agent, representing many award winners in television and film. She also taught three years for the UCLA Extension's Department of Entertainment Studies and Performing Arts. Victorya earned her bachelor's degree from California State University at Long Beach and her master's degree in theology from Fuller Theological Seminary. She speaks across the country helping singles make better choices in relationships. Victorya has been married to Will, her man worth keeping, for ten years and lives in a suburb of Dallas with her husband and two children, Matthew and Katie.

www.finderskeepersclub.com
www.victoryarogers.com

I'd Love to Hear from You!

Do you have a story to share or a comment to make about what you've learned in *The Automatic 2nd Date*? If so, I want to hear from you. You can reach me by visiting my Web sites or writing to me at my address below:

VICTORYA'S WEB SITES:
www.victorya.com
www.finderskeepersclub.com
www.myspace.com/victoryarogers

VICTORYA'S MAILING ADDRESS:
The Finder's Keepers Club
c/o Victorya Rogers Company
P.O. Box 92522
Southlake, TX 76092

You can also get my ongoing relationship advice and dating tips by visiting and subscribing to my blogs at:

VICTORYA'S BLOGS
www.blog.myspace.com/victoryarogers
www.victoryarogers.blogspot.com

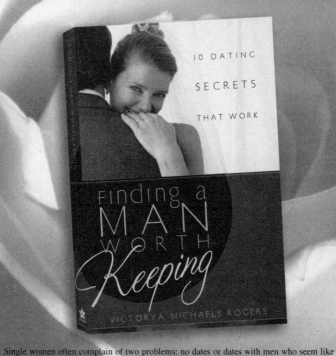